Praise for **Transforming Scho**

MW01068092

"The principles discussed in *Transforming Schools Through Systems Change* are effective and life changing. This book describes using personal connection, dedication, and determination to start the turnaround process. It is a must-read for any educator dedicated to making a difference in the success of their schoolhouse." — **Stephanie Lundberg**, principal, Holmes Elementary School

"This book gives us hope for developing an educational system that is effective and equitable for all students. We felt empowered by the defining of the systems and of the roles everyone plays. It is one of the first times in our careers that we felt like we are all in it together, working toward a common goal using the same map." — **Dixie Grunenfelder** and **Tim Stensager**, Washington State Office of Superintendent of Public Instruction

"*Transforming Schools Through Systems Change* is a must-read for all school administrators, teachers, and parents who are interested in learning about making real change happen. These systems allowed our high school to move from a graduation rate that was below fifty percent in 2007-08 to a rate of ninety percent in 2015." —**David Martinez**, assistant principal, Sunnyside High School

Transforming Schools Through Systems Change

Transforming Schools Through Systems Change

Charles Salina, Suzann Girtz,
and Joanie Eppinga

ROWMAN & LITTLEFIELD
Lanham • Boulder • New York • London

Published by Rowman & Littlefield
A wholly owned subsidiary of The Rowman & Littlefield Publishing Group, Inc.
4501 Forbes Boulevard, Suite 200, Lanham, Maryland 20706
www.rowman.com

Unit A, Whitacre Mews, 26-34 Stannary Street, London SE11 4AB

British Library Cataloguing in Publication Information Available

Library of Congress Cataloging-in-Publication Data

ISBN 978-1-4758-2231-1 (cloth : alk. paper) -- ISBN 978-1-4758-2232-8 (pbk. : alk. paper) -- ISBN 978-1-4758-2233-5 (electronic)

∞ ™ The paper used in this publication meets the minimum requirements of American National Standard for Information Sciences Permanence of Paper for Printed Library Materials, ANSI/NISO Z39.48-1992.

Printed in the United States of America

This book is dedicated to all the courageous servant-leader educators. These educators meet the needs of those they serve by creating a sense of belonging, empowering each person, building capacity and community, and grounding their work in social justice.

Contents

List of Figures

Foreword

It is no secret that our schools are struggling. That struggle is due, in part, to an organizational orientation that doesn't emphasize the importance of, as this book puts it, "creating a sense of belonging and power regarding the well-being of the group and the organization—the essence of servant-leadership."

A lifelong student of how things get done in organizations, Robert Greenleaf, the founder of servant-leadership, was especially concerned with encouraging the understanding and practice of servant-leadership within educational systems. Greenleaf examined the process of teaching/learning and offered his thinking on how servant-leadership could enhance the experiences of both students and teachers.

As Greenleaf so eloquently described the servant-leader in his seminal essay "The Servant as Leader,"

> It begins with the natural feeling that one wants to serve, to serve first. Then conscious choice brings one to aspire to lead. The difference manifests itself in the care taken by the servant— first to make sure that other people's highest priority needs are being served. The best test is: Do those served grow as persons; do they, while being served, become healthier, wiser, freer, more autonomous, more likely themselves to become servants?

And, what is the effect on the least privileged in society? Will
they benefit or at least not be further deprived?

This book offers an educational model for making sure that people's highest priority needs are being served. Among those needs
are a sense of belonging, of being able to contribute, and that others
also can and will contribute—what this book calls relational trust.
This trust suffuses the model presented here, allowing all parties to
become empowered and do their best work while serving others.

Greenleaf emphasized several characteristics salient to the process of servant-leadership, including listening, empathy, healing,
awareness, persuasion, conceptualization, foresight, stewardship,
commitment to the growth of people, and building community.
These ten characteristics of servant-leadership are by no means
exhaustive. However, they serve to communicate the power and
promise that this concept offers to accompanying servant-leaders
who are open to its invitation and challenge.

This book describes ways in which many of these characteristics
can be manifested in our schools—

Listening intently is of utmost importance as a foundation for
the one-on-one meetings the book advocates throughout.

Empathy, in which one recognizes others' special and unique
spirits and believes in them, is what allows all people in the school
to live out their dispensation, connect with their mission, and
understand their role in the organization.

Healing comes about when people no longer work in isolation,
or only in their departments, but trust that administrators, teachers,
and students will all bring something valuable to the table.

Awareness, which Greenleaf described as "a disturber and an
awakener," is addressed in this book through the notion that leaders
in schools must embrace conflict and see it as a way to move closer
to an ideal reality.

Conceptualization includes thinking beyond the day-to-day cri-
ses that can so easily absorb people working in education. Rather

than focusing only on putting out the fires that are always present in low-achieving schools, leaders must also allocate mental energy for moving closer to their envisioned reality. This characteristic is a potent element of the 45-day plan described within as a "call to action" and as school leaders' "lesson plan."

Commitment to the growth of people means empowering each person to play his or her role with heart and dedication. When this commitment is present, administrators believe in teachers and teachers believe in students. Everyone seeks to clear away any situational dross that keeps others from displaying their truest and most potent gifts. This commitment allows people the autonomy to take risks and supports them at times when plans are not realized.

Building community is one of the most important characteristics of servant-leadership, and of a powerful school. Community is built in schools by fostering relational trust. It grows when people declare their accountability to one another and when formal leaders get buy-in from their staffs about how to move the organization forward.

Greenleaf said, "All that is needed to rebuild community as a viable life form for large numbers of people is for enough servant-leaders to show the way, not by mass movements, but by each servant-leader demonstrating his or her own unlimited liability for a quite specific community-related group."

In many ways, the authors of this book have demonstrated their own "unlimited liability" for everyone associated with school systems. *Transforming Schools through Systems Change* provides a road map for helping to make servant-leadership a reality in school systems. I recommend what follows as a dynamic approach to the creation of servant-led schools everywhere.

Larry C. Spears
The Spears Center (Indianapolis)
Gonzaga University (Spokane)
Indianapolis, Indiana

January 2016

Larry C. Spears is author/editor of fifteen books on servant-leadership, including *Conversations on Servant-Leadership* (2015) and *Insights on Leadership* (1998). He is the editor of the five books of writings by Robert K. Greenleaf. Larry serves as Servant-Leadership Scholar for Gonzaga University's School for Professional Studies (Spokane), where he teaches graduate courses in servant-leadership and listening, and as Senior Advisory Editor for *The International Journal of Servant-Leadership*. He is also president of The Spears Center for Servant-Leadership (Indianapolis)—www.spearscenter.org. From 1990 to 2007, Larry served as president and chief executive officer of The Robert K. Greenleaf Center. A 2004 interview with him on NBC Dateline was seen by ten million viewers.

Acknowledgment

We deeply appreciate the significant contributions of Nina Neff-Mallon to the structure and clarity of this volume.

Introduction

The first Powerless to Powerful book, *Leadership for School Change*, outlined a vision for transitioning powerless, low-achieving schools into thriving, high-achieving schools. It told the remarkable story of Sunnyside High School, a struggling school where the graduation rate went from 49 percent to 85 percent in four years. The book also introduced the conceptual framework behind this transformation, which consisted of a unique combination of academic press, social support, and relational trust. These concepts, all implemented within a humanistic paradigm of servant-leadership, provide the groundwork for transforming a powerless school into a powerful school.

In this book, *Transforming Schools through Systems Change*, you will learn about the practical process of applying academic press, social support, and relational trust. This book talks about putting the ideas to work in a specific and actionable way. It offers a road map that shows you how to turn those ideas into systems that support the adults and students in the school as they all move toward higher academic achievement.

Much of the framework feels intuitive, like common sense; however, it has not led to common practice. The conceptual framework is easy to describe, but it's difficult to actualize if systems are not in place that facilitate each of its three elements. In other words, a culture that promotes the learning and growth of each member has to be intentionally developed through systems embedded in academic press, social support, and relational trust. Collaboration, evidence-based decision making, and systems of support aligned with the students' needs are the foundation for the road map detailed in this book in three sections, described below.

PART I: JOINING FORCES—MOVING TOWARD A COMMON GOAL

Joining forces is essential to transform a school from powerless to powerful, because when people work together toward a common goal they reconnect with their mission and relational trust flourishes. In low-performing schools, leaders can use what appear to be overwhelming barriers as opportunities to help staff change their beliefs about themselves, their students, their colleagues, and their schools by collaborating during the problem-solving process.

In Part I, we offer seven Opportunities, along with complementary Action Steps, that support teachers in effectively joining forces. We share strategies for learning to:

1. Drop Your Defenses
2. Re-Engage Teachers with Teachers
3. Clarify the Work
4. Declare Your Accountability to Each Other
5. Make Sense Through Action
6. Align Content and Instruction
7. Be Product Driven

Part I offers ways to develop these Opportunities and gives step-by-step Action Steps to use as you encourage staff to join forces using the conceptual framework discussed in our first book. When collaboration permeates the school, an atmosphere of unity, focus, and curiosity is created that fosters relational trust. For that reason, what others call Professional Learning Communities, or PLCs, we call Collaborative Inquiry teams, or *CoIn teams*.

CoIn teams meet regularly to problem solve and apply action research to difficulties related to their discipline, and to make sure their actions align with schoolwide systems. These teams are vital to the health of powerful schools because they constitute the first step in supporting the collaboration that develops relational trust.

PART II: THE SUCCESS TEAM—APPLYING THE CONCEPTUAL FRAMEWORK

To be powerful, a school needs a team of professionals that can apply the conceptual framework systemically. Often such a team, which we call a Success Team, consists largely or solely of school counselors; however, schools that have few or no counselors can draw on other professionals already in the building, redefining their roles and reapportioning their duties to allow them to participate. We'll speak primarily of counselors, but keep in mind that specialists, learning coaches, and others can be assigned roles on the Success Team.

Success Team members are vital in implementing systems that are grounded in the conceptual framework. In a powerless school, counselors often wait for students to seek them out. Problems pile up, and counselors are constantly putting out fires. In a powerful school, the role of the counselor (or other Success Team member) is reframed, and the counselors' duties are reprioritized. Counselors spend more time out in the field, where they support teachers and students through aligned systems designed to address their individual needs.

Part II details how Success Team members realize student success in their schools using a comprehensive, evidence-based program. This program changes things up. Counselors collaborate with each other, with administrators, with teachers, and with parents. Additionally, they and other Success Team members advocate for every student, helping each one to achieve academic goals through systemic support.

PART III: SCHOOLWIDE SYSTEMS—PUTTING IT ALL TOGETHER

Part III is the most nuts-and-bolts part of the book—it's where we describe specific systems designed to help a school succeed. These systems are tailored to increasing levels of intervention, and within each level are programs structured to target three critical areas: behavior management, social-emotional development, and academic achievement.

The systems detailed in Part III include a lunchtime tutoring program, a peer-to-peer mentoring program, a credit retrieval program, and many others. The goal of these programs is to provide a framework for the three efforts that are essential for creating a powerful school:

- Connecting students to the school;
- Helping them to envision their futures; and
- Building powerful relationships.

The programs outlined are suggestions culled from our experience in transforming schools, and leaders will need to adapt them for their individual schools. If they do so, they will be creating the organizational climate that is at the heart of servant-leadership: an atmosphere in which all employees and students, and eventually the organization itself, can become stronger in a context of caring relationships.

I

Joining Forces—Moving Toward a Common Goal

Part I breaks down various factors that contribute to isolationism in schools and offers ways to bring the people in a schoolhouse together.

Talk of shifting instructional practice is common. What we want to make clear is that if teachers are to change their instructional practices, they must first be able to take an honest look at themselves and their beliefs about their students, their colleagues, their schools, and their role in the organization—without feeling shamed or blamed. It's up to leaders to create the appropriate atmosphere for self-reflection that will eventually lead to changes in instructional practice.

The work of Collaborative Inquiry (CoIn) is most effective when leaders who have a vision direct change with an emphasis on solving problems. They need to clarify that change can't take place only on an individual level—it must take place through colleagues joining forces as they seek answers.

It's up to leaders to create an environment where people work together, and they do so by demonstrating new behaviors. Those new behaviors start to shift teachers' beliefs about what is acceptable and possible; then opportunities open up for them to re-engage

1

with their mission within a culture for learning that is grounded in the inquiry practice. The result is transformational learning—for everyone in the schoolhouse.

Transformational learning that takes place through CoIn is most effective when it's grounded in new leadership behaviors based on the conceptual framework of academic press, social support, and relational trust. Those behaviors were discussed in *Powerless to Powerful: Leadership for School Change*, and they are further developed here. This book—and particularly this section—elaborates upon how school leaders can capitalize on opportunities to change and improve schools. Both books emphasize the primacy of relational trust.

Relational trust acts as both a catalyst for and an outcome of the union of academic press and social support. Relational trust grows because roles and responsibilities have been clarified in an environment where people have high expectations, believe that each other will perform, and feel sure that support will be provided (Bryk & Schneider, 2003).

In that situation, people are more willing to be held accountable for the steps along the way as they move collaboratively toward mutually held organizational goals. Getting all stakeholders to be willing to be held accountable for the goals of the school promotes a culture for learning. Figure 1.1 illustrates the nature of the relationships among academic press, social support, and relational trust that promote learning. This conceptual framework applies to all levels of interactions within the schoolhouse, regardless of age or role.

Before we move on to our specific road map, here is a quick review of the conceptual framework:

Academic press provides specific academic direction embedded in high standards/goals and in the belief that everyone can achieve success.

Social support is the provision of emotional and academic support that allows students to succeed.

Relational trust is the mutual and interdependent respect that results when people feel safe, believe that everyone has something to offer, and are confident that each person is willing to offer the time and expertise necessary for movement toward success.

Culture changes take place when questions related to academic press and social support are being asked simultaneously, and when behaviors and beliefs are rooted in relational trust. Figure 1.1 illustrates this dynamic.

As the circles of academic press and social support begin to overlap, a culture shift takes place that supports and challenges everyone to learn and to be their best selves.

Figure 1.1 Conceptual framework.

This relationship among each of the factors found in the conceptual framework is what leads to a powerful culture shift in a school that feels powerless. This framework is embedded in all aspects of the work that happens within the schoolhouse. As a result of stakeholders embracing this framework, people *connect to the school, develop positive relationships, and envision their future.* Creating this atmosphere should be a welcome challenge for leaders.

This section discusses, within the context of low-performing schools, how leaders can use what appear to be overwhelming barriers as opportunities to succeed in helping staff change their beliefs about themselves, their students, their colleagues, and their schools—a mindset of seeing challenges as opportunity sometimes known as embracing "positive opposites." Teachers with this mindset learn to drop their fear of the current reality in favor of embracing the challenges of turning around a low-performing school through a collaborative process embedded in the constructs of academic press, social support, and relational trust.

OPPORTUNITY #1: DROP YOUR DEFENSES

Leadership is the catalyst for improved learning. Formal leaders who long to light the fuse of change and harness the power of collaboration drop all defensiveness and declare first *what* they *are willing to be held accountable for. Only then will teachers engage in conversations about what* they *are willing to be held accountable for.*

In a powerless school, teachers are wary of being blamed for low student achievement. Because they often do not believe themselves or their colleagues to be capable of collective problem solving, they are likely to place blame for schoolhouse failure on poverty, parents, administrators, or the students themselves. Because they do not feel psychologically safe or empowered to effect change, teachers strike a defensive pose.

In this defensive posture, teachers develop a sense of learned helplessness because they aren't offered the support necessary for them to be effective. It's hard for a person who feels ineffective to be committed to making a difference. Such teachers are likely to shut down as a result of feeling inadequate to meet the needs of their students. Many teachers who feel powerless may not have the skill set to move forward in the CoIn process. Why would teachers want to collaborate when it appears that the work of the CoIn team is nothing more than a waste of time?

Administrators need to get out in front of the blame game to neutralize learned helplessness. Effective formal leaders are sensitive to the fact that teachers are already laboring under an immense weight of frustration and responsibility for students' failures—and leaders do what they can to alleviate those feelings among teachers. Administrators aren't paid large sums of money merely to work hard. They're paid to be accountable and take the heat. Powerful leaders let teachers know: "If you fail, I have failed you." Powerful superintendents offer the same message to their principals.

Formal leaders can respond to teacher defensiveness by engaging in action steps to jumpstart the CoIn process in a way that allows teachers to reengage. At the same time, effective leaders develop schoolwide systems intended to support teachers regarding the behavioral and achievement needs of students—*before* the actual CoIn process is in place.

It is important to note that although these steps are presented in an order, the process of change is not linear. It is complex and requires multiple simultaneous efforts. For clarity, we have presented a process, but we do not want to imply that the process is a simple matter of ordered steps. With that said, the following steps do describe potential primary efforts in the change process.

Action Steps for Dropping Your Defenses

1. Use a statement similar to the one that follows as a springboard for initiating a conversation that doesn't blame teachers for a school's low achievement rates.

> Teachers are on the front lines, and principals provide the foundation for their work. Leaders offer teachers support and provide them with relevant information that allows them to be effective. If students aren't learning, formal leaders need to take the responsibility and acknowledge that they have not supported teachers sufficiently.

With this defensiveness-alleviating statement as a starting point, engage in conversations with teachers, both one-on-one and in small groups. This conversation is grounded in teachers' collective, face-saving assertion that the problem lies in the lack of the right kind of external support for their work. The reality is, the teachers are right!

2. Declare up front to everyone that you, the leaders, are accountable for teachers' success and the success of the school. Make no mistake: Leaders are there to ensure the success of the school staff through the creation of systems and processes that make the school a learning organization. Own this and repeat it. Convey a strong belief that each student and teacher can be successful in the classroom.

3. Initiate one-on-one discussions with teachers about their perceptions regarding areas in which leaders could more effectively support them in their work. Don't get sidetracked by the venting and anger. Focus on the real message, which typically centers on having too many students who come to school unprepared to learn (achievement), students who act out or don't come to school (behavior), and too many students who are suffering the effects of trauma (social-emotional). Teachers need to know that the school

has support systems to assist not only these students, but the work of the staff. Those systems are described in part III.

Organize the staff members' feedback into big ideas or themes that emerged from the one-on-one conversations about what they need and expect from the leadership. These themes are likely to be related to the three realms of systems development (behavioral, academic, and social-emotional). Present the results of your conversations, these themes, to the faculty. Check in with teachers, both one-on-one and in group meetings, to see if you have it right. Be open and keep your defenses down in order to avoid the elbow-lock tendencies of people attempting to push back by explaining or rationalizing. Just listen. Absorb and embrace the teachers' perceptions in such a way that staff members feel assured that the *conversation will turn into action.* Resist the temptation to discuss teachers' instructional practices at this point. Keep the focus on school-wide issues and leadership behaviors. Embrace the teachers' frustration—use it and their ideas to move the school forward.

4. Bring collective findings back to the faculty. No one should be surprised by them, because as a formal leader you will have done your homework and conducted your important one-on-one conversations. Collect specific evidence on attendance, tardies, discipline referrals, and the number of students passing all of their classes. Emphasize what schoolwide systems (rather than teachers) can do to address these issues. The role of schoolwide systems will be addressed further in part III.

5. Implement essential schoolwide systems to support teacher and student learning, with these discussions as the groundwork. Parts II and III offer context for how to conduct this process. A sense of a new beginning will begin to arise as the leadership formally declares that they are willing to be held *accountable*, thereby creating a culture for learning through schoolwide systems. Point out clearly how the taking of responsibility by leadership relates to the statement offered in Action Step 1.

6. Make teacher thinking evident in a leadership lesson plan, which was referred to in *Powerless to Powerful: Leadership for School Change* as "the 45-day plan" and will be further explored at the end of this book. Share the plan publicly and return to it often.

7. On an ongoing basis, remind teachers that as a leader you are accountable for their success, just as they are accountable for their students' success. Put this out there routinely—even weekly—and ask for ongoing feedback on the systems and processes being implemented. Make sure teachers can see that their feedback results in leaders taking *real action* to support their work.

As a result of the leaders' actions, teachers feel valued and relational trust begins to form. As teachers see that leaders have something to offer and that they are willing to put in the time and effort to provide real help, this trust grows. The process of teachers coming to feel safe will be ongoing, given that leaders will need to continually demonstrate that trying new behaviors to support learning is more important than achieving immediate success.

SUMMARY:

When administrators declare what they are willing to be held accountable for, teachers become more willing to drop their defenses because they perceive that formal leaders are working in alignment with them toward common goals. When leaders take in, organize, and disseminate information in a way that built as everyone works to promote student success.

OPPORTUNITY #2: REENGAGE TEACHERS WITH TEACHERS

Two-way communication between teachers is essential if teaching and learning are to improve. Building the belief that "to-

gether, we will accomplish great things" begins when teachers support teachers.

When leaders listen to teachers' feedback about what they can do schoolwide to support teaching and learning, they take an important step toward helping teachers feel safe enough to reengage in the work of the school. Formal leaders model the way, showing vulnerability in accepting feedback and willingness to change behaviors to meet the needs of those served.

Ensuring that teachers feel safe with each other, have something to offer each other, and are willing to take time to help each other requires the use of structured processes directed by administrators. When formal leaders show a willingness to be held accountable for teacher success, the process of teachers engaging in conversations about their work together *unfolds over a few weeks, not months.* Effective formal leaders send a message: "The work we are all doing together is primary." Once leaders have delivered the message through their actions that change is happening, they do well to maintain a focus on that message; other concerns can't take priority. This is the work, right now.

People often say that school change is slow. Not all aspects of it need to be slow—in fact, some need to take place with urgency. Leaders are the ones to make the change happen. Their job is to start processes simultaneously and manage them in a way that is visible, which will result in people within the schoolhouse responding with enthusiasm and hopefulness.

As formal leaders discuss how they're attempting to demonstrate new behaviors in being accountable for teachers' success, they share with teachers a non-negotiable: *Collaboration is not optional* (DuFour, 2004). Implied in this non-negotiable is that through collaboration, collective agreements are made regarding leaders' belief in the capability of teachers and students. As administrators step forward and acknowledge that they are responsible for the success of teachers, the teachers take on that same responsibility for the success of students.

Also implied in this statement is an understanding of the power of public reflection. As DuFour and Eaker noted in 1998, the essence of learning teams' work is getting teachers to become willing to declare what they collectively think regarding which content should be taught to students (resulting in common learning outcomes) and how they will know whether students have learned (through common formative and summative assessments).

Powerless to Powerful: Leadership for School Change discusses the role of teacher self-efficacy in student learning. When teachers believe they are effective, they really *are* more effective. They contribute to student learning and have authority in their classrooms.

Effective leaders are aware of collective efficacy—that is, of how individual teachers perceive that their colleagues, as a group, are able to effect student learning and manage student behavior. *In effective CoIn teams, collective efficacy is developed as teachers mutually support each other in improving teaching practices.* Teacher efficacy increases due to improved student learning and, in turn, student efficacy increases, which produces still higher student achievement.

When teachers engage in conversations about these topics, they begin to publicly frame in the components for which they are willing to be held accountable. It's important that their thinking be public, for two reasons: (a) it puts their thinking front and center, which allows leaders to continually emphasize its importance; and (b) it prevents teachers from withholding their thinking about these issues, which they cannot be allowed to do because such withholding is destructive and can tear down the team.

As teachers present their thinking publicly, it's important that they feel safe—and that sense of safety is the responsibility of the formal leaders. Effective leaders help their staff understand: As long as they're *working on* figuring out what it is that students should know and what the evidence of that knowledge will look like, it's okay if they don't yet know the answers to those questions. Having those answers isn't essential as long as all teachers know that both they and their colleagues have something to offer and are working collaboratively toward a common goal.

Powerful leaders model the fact that they too may not yet have specific answers. It is often scary to move from the known to the unknown. In this process of trying to answer the questions, achieving the goal is not the only focus. If that process is conducted correctly, relational trust will grow.

It's most productive to have the formal leader be the one who shapes the nature of the conversation that leads to a collaborative culture. Having outside consultants lead the conversations only reinforces the conviction that the solution does not lie within. For that reason, effective formal leaders do their homework on how to lead a process like the one described in the Action Steps that follow.

Sometimes staff members may be polite to one another or engage in friendly small talk, but that doesn't mean they're truly joining forces. In a low-performing school, staff members are sometimes barely civil. To promote true collaboration, effective leaders convey that difficult issues will be confronted directly. Directness helps staff have faith in the protocols and processes that are in place for solving problems.

These protocols are embedded in the conceptual framework—leaders take time to describe clearly the current reality by providing evidence as supported by contextual and perceptual data. As the current reality is described, a collective ideal is created. The school climate at this time may be stormy, but leaders must be courageous enough to weather rough seas. They must develop a culture for learning that helps the school persevere through a poor climate as stakeholders embrace a sense of hopefulness and continue moving toward the ideal.

The Action Steps are grounded in Lencioni's Five Dysfunctions of an Organization. A brief review of Lencioni's work, as discussed in *Powerless to Powerful: Leadership for School Change*, is offered in the following paragraphs, followed by the related activities to re-engage teachers.

Lencioni's team assessment tool[1] allows leaders to diagnose the readiness of the teams to benefit in each of his five areas of organizational development: developing trust, embracing conflict, building commitments, being accountable, and obtaining meaningful results. This tool begins a conversation with a staff that feels powerless, allowing team members to dig deeply into the development of relational trust and to understand the nature of conflict.

Many of the attributes described in the Five Dysfunctions are present in a school that feels powerless. People don't trust each other. Students are not considered capable, administrators do not believe in staff, and certain factions of the staff don't have faith in each other's abilities. In such a situation, what would make staff willing to talk about how they interact with each other and how to build accountability?

In schools lacking a sense of power, frustrations are high due to the failure rate, and the ability to solve problems is significantly diminished. People feel alone in their efforts to achieve the goals of the organization, and that sense of isolation results in deep-seated fear regarding commitment to and accountability for new "agreements" that feel as if they come from the top down rather than being agreed upon by the group. If dysfunctions are not addressed within a school in which people feel powerless, the school not only will continue to lack power, but will also become broken.

Administrators are sometimes reluctant to focus on dysfunctional processes in their schools because they fear conflict, or because they are afraid that they reflect on their inability to lead. Consequently, they run from conflict rather than embracing the possibility of positive opposites. Leaders working for change do well to remember the three rules of leadership:

- Accept that conflict is part of the job.
- Embrace ambiguity.
- Have faith that if systems are structured correctly, people will do the right thing and self-correct.

These rules can all be employed to address team dysfunctions. If they are not addressed, it is highly unlikely that staff will engage in collaboration in the CoIn process.

Action Steps for Getting Teachers to Reengage With Teachers

1. Assign teachers to their department and or grade-level CoIn teams. Create a CoIn team of their own for specialists, such as counselors, psychologists, and learning coaches. If there are fewer than four individuals, combine teams with complementary jobs. For example, career teachers and technical teachers may form one CoIn team. This step of assigning teams is critical to think through within the context of your school's needs. Don't be afraid to ask staff what these teams may look like.

2. Introduce the staff to results of research on functional and dysfunctional organizations. As mentioned earlier, having the formal leader of the building provide this mini-lesson is much more powerful than bringing in an outside consultant.

3. Have each learning team fill out Lencioni's assessment that measures various dysfunctions as the staff perceive them, *schoolwide*. Collect the teachers' surveys and tabulate them. Use the mean, median, and mode in tabulating the data. Post the school data publicly to the staff; bring it out regularly for review and updates. CoIn data can also be confined to its particular group in terms of how they perceive schoolwide dysfunctions, so they can periodical-

ly share with the staff to get differing perceptions. By the end of the first year, you may outgrow this process and want to visit it less regularly.

4. Now have the teachers fill in the survey regarding how they perceive the effectiveness of *their own CoIn teams* in the context of the five dysfunctions. Have each learning team tabulate their results, again using the mean, median, and mode.

5. Share the schoolwide results. Give teachers time to discuss the findings in their CoIn teams. Make it clear as a leadership team that it is important for teachers to openly share their thinking behind the scores. Let them know that this type of feedback allows formal leaders to learn new behaviors about showing what they are accountable for and improving school culture.

6. Give teachers ample time to discuss their findings as they relate to their CoIn teams. Have them ask themselves and each other this question: "Are we congenial or collaborative as it pertains to each of the five dysfunctions within our team?" In other words, are we superficially friendly and coming to superficial agreements, or are we digging deep to find genuine answers as a team? It may take time to move from congenial to collaborative, but staff must move from compliance to commitment.

7. Have CoIn teams compare and contrast their team's mean and mode scores for each dysfunction with the schoolwide mean and mode. Again, make this data public by posting it visibly. Note: This step may bring out pain within the staff and/or the team. Just as teachers are frustrated with the leadership in a low-performing school, they are frustrated with each other as well.

8. Explain to the staff that the schoolwide and department/grade score from the survey is a baseline. It will become a metric they will use to hold themselves accountable in regaining belief in each other so they can move forward and find ways to hold each other accountable, thereby achieving new results. In the first year of re-

engaging staff, revisit schoolwide and department/grade-level scorecards quarterly.

9. Throughout the process, continue to do regular one-on-ones with staff to gain feedback about what the data is telling them and what actions they perceive as necessary to move to a new ideal. This data provides tremendous insight as CoIn teams begin their journey of collective problem solving.

SUMMARY:

Effective leaders model vulnerability and fearlessly address dysfunction to encourage teachers to support and engage with one another. No excuses are acceptable for not joining forces with colleagues.

OPPORTUNITY #3: CLARIFY THE WORK

Creating a collective purpose statement for the collaborative inquiry team's work provides both motivation and a framework for understanding how the strengths of each person fit into the well-being of the organization.

By now the formal leaders have made it clear that joining forces is key to success. They have clearly stated what they are accountable for and have engaged in new behaviors, described in *Powerless to Powerful: Leadership for School Change*, that build trust. Trust is further developed by defining what is *important to staff*. Identifying the collective purpose of their CoIn teams will motivate staff to engage in the work of those teams. Clarity of purpose motivates people to engage in the work. People get burned out when they are engaged in work that takes them away from their mission, such as meaningless workshops or additional reporting systems.

Clarity of purpose is supported by Greenleaf's 1970 theory of servant-leadership. Leaders who align with that theory:

- Ensure that other people's highest order needs are being met, thereby developing a sense of belonging.
- Are committed to the growth of people. Leaders build capacity by believing in others and by working to their strengths, interests, and needs.
- Inspire others to lead, whereupon they become servant-leaders themselves.
- Embed their efforts in social justice. (p. 6)

Effective conversations on this topic center on three things: (a) formal leadership's responsibility for creating a culture for learning that is safe and supports the teachers' work; (b) formal leaders' belief that their teachers have the capacity to do this work; and (c) formal leadership's clarity about how each person's talents contribute to the work.

A collective purpose allows everyone to make sense of the work and to align their efforts with the goals of the school and the district. This alignment creates an avenue for coherence, thereby enhancing learning goals and instructional practice and reducing the experience of being fractured and overloaded. It provides focus and delimits the work, making it less likely that people will perceive their workload as being overwhelming or a meaningless add-on task sent from above.

What seems obvious may not be so to those in a low-achieving school. Often, a fractured staff has lost sight of their collective mission, so they double down on efforts to live out their individual roles. Thus, individuals become activity driven and a culture of busy-ness becomes pervasive.

Devising a purpose statement for staff's work as a CoIn team is an important step in moving toward goal-driven work; however, it doesn't guarantee action. Once clarity of purpose is established and team norms are developed, teams have increased their opportunity to authentically assess their potential for dysfunction.

The best way to get teachers to begin engaging in collective problem solving is to have them declare, one by one, what provides purpose for them in doing their individual work and then develop a group CoIn purpose statement. The leadership team also prepares a collective purpose statement that they share with the other CoIn teams. In this way, they transparently demonstrate how that work supports the well-being of the organization.

When implementing the Action Steps below, be sure to keep making the survey results from Opportunity #2 visible as a reminder that, through these conversations, staff can build trust if they embrace their differences while they develop common commitments.

Action Steps for Clarifying the Work

1. Review the missions of the district and the school. In their CoIn teams, teachers discuss how these missions are or are not aligned. Teachers may find it helpful to discuss the key words that drive the beliefs embedded in each of the statements. List these words so they are visible.

2. In their CoIn teams, have the teachers respond in writing to the following question: *What is it that gives your professional life purpose and meaning?*

Have teachers share their purpose statements. Identify common power words and actions that support those statements. Discuss how each of the purpose statements supports the mission of the school and the district. Ask teachers to share stories about how they see each other living their purpose statement. Celebrate what people are saying and doing, remembering that *slower is faster* in terms of having teachers take the time in their CoIn teams to *publicly* catch each other doing things that bring them closer to realizing the collective mission. Celebrate those moments.

3. Provide the CoIn teams with a brief overview of the three central ideas for a learning team as described by DuFour: keeping learning as the focus, committing to working together, and assessing effectiveness based on results. Allow time for CoIn teams to discuss each of these ideas and how it relates to their work. Additionally, have the teams describe how these principles support their purpose statement and the mission of the school and district.

Aligning each CoIn team's personal purpose statement with the district's and school's mission is important work. Allow time for team members to talk about how each of the behaviors previously discussed supports the well-being of the school and its students, making it clear how each person's strengths contribute to the overall success of the organization. Again, find a way that works for your school to celebrate, both privately and publicly, the work that people are doing. Sometimes it may be more powerful to celebrate privately with an individual, depending on that person's temperament.

4. Develop a collective purpose statement for each CoIn learning team. This is the time to define the nature of the work. The purpose statement declares the group's *true north*, to use Stephen Covey's (2013) term, or *why* they are engaging in this work. The following steps are helpful in creating a collective CoIn purpose statement:

- Have each person on the learning team write down one to three sentences to complete the following prompt: "The purpose of our CoIn team is to ____." Share the results.
- Instruct the members as follows: "Silently read each person's purpose statement. As you read each one, underline any power words or phrases that speak to you; you may underline as many words on each person's purpose statement as you would like. You may underline a word even if someone else has already underlined that word."
- Now list any words that have at least half as many underlines as there are participants in the group. For example, if you have six

people in your group, then any word that has three or more lines under it would be placed on the paper.

- If anyone's purpose statement has a word that did not receive the requisite number of underlines but that the author feels is very important, the author may discuss that word with the group, and, if consensus is reached, that word may be placed on the paper.
- Using as many of the power words as possible, compose a group purpose statement (Adapted from Glasser, *The Quality School*, 1998).

5. At the end of the exercise, have each CoIn team write their collective purpose statement. Have one member of the group read the statement, first to one another to increase their sense of safety, and later to the assembled staff. Post each of the purpose statements alongside the schoolwide survey findings, for both the school as a whole and the CoIn teams. Have each learning team discuss their collective purpose statement and how the survey informs the nature of the work going forward.

6. Observe aloud that this purpose statement defines each learning team's true north and is the first step in their becoming collectively accountable for the efforts they make to improve their work. Examples of such purpose statements follow.

> The purpose of our learning team is to collaborate using different forms of data, including emotional and social information, to empower staff and students to continually learn and grow in a supportive and encouraging environment. (elementary teachers' CoIn team)

> Our purpose as a team is to collaborate to discuss learning outcomes, instruction, and learning strategies to help improve student achievement; to consistently work to create and maintain an equitable, respectful, and supportive environment for our teachers and students. (secondary teachers' team)

The purpose of our learning team is to work together to support students and teachers in order to help them meet their goals, specifically high school graduation and plans beyond, through effective monitoring systems. (counselors' CoIn team)

As a leadership team, we are intentional in our behaviors so that our work of initiating, monitoring, and evaluating schoolwide goals and actions that will support teaching and learning will ensure higher student achievement and increased graduation rates. (formal leaders' CoIn team)

7. Keep these purpose statements clearly visible in a place where the faculty frequently congregate. A later section will describe how to return to these statements, review the process, and keep a "score-card" to monitor success.

SUMMARY:

Developing a public purpose statement is a collaborative action that builds teamwork and allows all persons to clarify how they individually fit into the overall and sustainable plan of the schoolhouse.

OPPORTUNITY #4: DECLARE YOUR ACCOUNTABILITY TO EACH OTHER

After creating a purpose statement, teachers and leaders answer this question: What behaviors do we need to demonstrate with each other to ensure that we actualize our purpose?

Much has been written about how to develop collective agreements, so Opportunity 4 will only briefly review highlights before offering suggestions regarding process.

DuFour refers to collective agreements as *team norms*. Staff's readiness to engage in discussions that result in agreement is more likely to be authentic if they have developed a collective purpose *before* shaping team norms. Team norms declare the behaviors they will collectively demonstrate to actualize their CoIn purpose statement.

Maintaining a focus on that purpose is the responsibility of leaders. School change won't happen if leaders aren't intentional, attentive, and willing to model the practices they advocate. Once these behaviors become the norm, they will spread to others and create concentric circles of sustainable progress.

Because team norms are created for the department and/or grade level, *are not schoolwide agreements*, and are grounded in the team's purpose statement, they have a much greater chance of being actualized. Many strategies or protocols have been put forth for establishing such norms, so just one example process for effectively establishing such norms is provided here.

According to Joan Richardson (1999) of the National Staff Development Council, formalizing team norms helps create groups that are able to have honest discussions, enabling everyone to participate and be heard. An adapted National Staff Development Council process, available at www.powerless2powerful.com, is very effective in working with low-performing schools.

Action Steps for Declaring Your Accountability

1. Ask each CoIn team to take a moment and reflect on their beliefs and behaviors that support their school's mission and their collective purpose statement. Ask: "How can we as a group demonstrate new behaviors to change our beliefs about each other and support the mission of our school?"

2. Remind each CoIn team: All team norms are intended to ensure that "all individuals have the opportunity to contribute in the meeting, to increase productivity and effectiveness, and to facilitate the achievement of its [the team's] purpose and goals" (Richardson, 1999, p. 3).

3. Reflect on National Staff Development Council questions about developing norms. Teams often generate common expectations within the areas of time use, listening, confidentiality, decision making, participation, and expectations. Responding to a few prompts that clarify each area can support the creation of a list of team norms that can be returned to on a regular basis to promote functional CoIn team processes.

4. As teams develop norms, they are creating a scorecard for behaviors that team members expect of each other. Have the teams evaluate the implementation of norms, initially on a weekly basis and then, once they are well established, monthly. Figure 1.2 shows a purpose statement from a CoIn team at one school that was in the process of moving from powerless to powerful. It includes an example of an actual scorecard used to report results.

5. As CoIn team members become more trusting and provide authentic feedback to each other, have them reduce the expected behaviors to a letter grade—because grades are a language that teachers understand, and giving them starts a conversation, which is the purpose of the scorecard. Talk about specific behaviors that support the grade.

In one school, team members initially gave themselves only A's and B's in an effort to be congenial. Finally the day came when enough relational trust had been established that they could say, "We gave ourselves an F this week. But it's okay, because we know what we need to do to get that grade up, and this work we do in the CoIn teams is important to us." At that point, the conversation had become both interesting and productive.

6. Once a month, in a traditional faculty meeting, have staff and administrators assess and report publicly on their progress toward achieving their collective purpose statement and living their group norms.

As clarity of collective CoIn team purpose and norms are developed and lived, relational trust is being developed. People feel safe,

The purpose of our CoIn team is to use action research to continuously move from our current reality to our collective ideal using agreed-upon evidence to ensure that our students are successful.

Team Norms	What do we do well?	What could we do better?
TIME: We will begin and end on time, and honor our agenda during the meeting.		
LISTENING: We will listen to each other and remain engaged throughout each meeting.		
TONE/ACTION ORIENTATION: We will maintain a positive tone, promising to complain only if we can offer a solution.		

Figure 1.2 Sample CoIn team purpose statement and scorecard.

know that they and others have something to offer, and believe that others will put in time and effort to help them.

SUMMARY:

Use team norms to develop a scorecard that allows each member of the team to assess whether the team members are moving toward their goals, collectively and individually. Use the scorecard to develop the concepts of building relational trust and becoming accountable.

OPPORTUNITY #5: MAKING SENSE THROUGH ACTION

Effective CoIn teams gather evidence to help them assess their current reality. They then use that evidence to move toward the ideal reality. Designing the research questions themselves allows them to buy in to the answers, which then inform their practice.

The primary focus of the CoIn process is to ensure that there is equity for students in the teaching and learning process. However, in low-performing schools that focus only on achievement data without considering different forms of evidence, systems change will be difficult to achieve.

Teachers who are seeking answers in low-performing schools are often driven toward quick fixes and look for programs rather than systems to support their work. Leaders may likewise bring in programs that they, or a select group of teachers, perceive as being relevant and necessary; but introducing programs doesn't necessarily mean they'll meet people's needs.

This is why it's important to help teachers become knowledgeable about action research, so that they move toward a deeper understanding grounded in evidence within their own contexts rather than toward new programs that claim to provide immediate results but actually offer nothing more than random activities.

Action research is focused on the problem at hand, meant to serve the people in your setting. Those involved in solving the problem devise strategies for collecting and analyzing evidence, interpreting the evidence, and implementing plans based on the evidence to address the problem. Buy-in tends to be high because the people in the field are the ones who design the research and act on the results. It allows practitioners to reflect on their practices and to respond intentionally.

We have learned in our work that applying the principles of action research will deepen teachers' thinking within their CoIn teams. Along those lines, Mertler (2012) described action research as a cyclical process of inquiry in which teams ask a question, gather data, and then use the data gathered to evaluate and shape the next research question, all with the purpose of improving the *context* for the people being served.

Although it may be embedded in the school change effort, action research by its very definition leads to doing business in a new way—new behaviors change old beliefs of both adults and students, leading to a commitment to *collectively* achieve better outcomes.

If CoIn is primarily result driven, typically it might focus exclusively on achievement data. Often demographic, perceptual, and contextual data is overlooked during the collaborative process. Action research requires that *each* form of evidence be collected and analyzed to improve teaching and learning.

For example, in one school, teachers were dutifully working to implement improved assessment practices that aligned with departmental learning targets. Achievement data, with which teachers were all too familiar, indicated that students were not learning the desired outcomes.

However, perceptual data indicated that teachers (and administrators) did not believe students would be able to meet learning expectations—and Hattie's 2009 research shows that teacher belief is a critical factor affecting whether students do in fact meet learning expectations. Perceptual data from the school also suggested that relational trust between teachers and students was low. Finally, contextual data revealed that few systems were present that would support students in achieving these targets.

It was critical for staff to have discussions between themselves and with formal leaders about how to apply the new assessments aligned with common learning outcomes within the context of school systems. The results of such a discussion led to the creation of schoolwide and departmental systems to support teachers and students in meeting the new expected outcomes. This dynamic approach allowed for change to take place at all levels—not just within a given classroom.

The process of delving deeply using the principles of action research led to a culture shift that increased the belief that students could learn (*academic press*) with specific supports (*social support*) in place. Consequently, both learning *and relational trust* increased.

Administrators often give teachers only academic data, and that is not enough to help teachers make sense of the work. Teachers need to be able to view students in a richer, more textured context. Unfortunately, when data is overcomplicated, it can be used as an excuse rather than a call to action. For example, often demographic data is seen as inevitably condemning a student to low achievement. However, action research that triangulates multiple forms of data will lead to an intentional action plan to move forward.

In professional development situations, external experts tell teachers, "This is what's important, and this is how you do it." That approach denies teachers the autonomy to develop a deep understanding and application of expected outcomes to enhance student achievement. The CoIn process not only allows teachers to make sense of the work but also adds clarity about what they are willing to be accountable for.

Frequently, formal leaders, including those at the district office level, work in isolation and prescribe what the schools and teachers need to do be successful. In the Effective Schools research conducted in the 1970s, Lezotte, Brookover, and Edmonds reminded us that the *schoolhouse* is the unit of change. This is still true today! However, without district support, the change at the building level is not sustainable and requires districts to use data in different ways that support equity at all levels. The bottom line is: They are all our students.

Applying the conceptual framework that supports the perceptions, demographics, and context of a given school allows the CoIn process to act on the needs of those being served. It creates a sense of belonging and power regarding the well-being of the group and the organization—the essence of servant-leadership.

The process of action research begins by identifying the group's current reality in terms of a specific problem and then envisioning a collective ideal to work toward. The group works to nail down exactly what the current situation is, what the problem is to be addressed, and what needs to be known about it. Before a cultural shift in thinking can be made, evidence about the current reality must be collected.

The current reality may be grounded in an achievement issues, such as low performance on a common departmental assessment. Quite often the immediate answer to such a problem is improved instructional practices—which may or may not be the solution, but is usually where people look regardless. The problem may be grounded in curriculum alignment, or behavioral/social-emotional needs, or specific learning needs such as those of English language learners. The gap between the current and the ideal scenario provides space for planning action steps.

After collecting evidence, at times CoIn team members may suffer from analysis paralysis and overthink or overdiscuss the different forms of data, without taking corresponding action. Effective analysis of data requires having the ability to categorize and to look for general themes and patterns.

This data does not take months to analyze. Resist the temptation to overhypothesize about what the data is telling you. Data *informs* decisions rather than drives them. The human element drives decisions regarding what is next based on the evidence and the related theme(s). The brain searches for themes and patterns. Identification of themes allows for sensemaking in determining a plan of action. The key is to use evidence to move to action that in turn will result in evidence that you'll collect to see whether you have moved closer to the new ideal and to inform what comes next as you identify themes related to the issue at hand.

At each step, CoIn teams collect and review the necessary forms of evidence (contextual, demographic, perceptual, achievement) to determine what steps to take and whether they're making progress toward the ideal (see Figure 1.3). Their work is aligned within the larger 45-day leadership plan. Thus the result may be improved instruction as well as schoolwide systems that support academic, social-emotional, and behavioral needs of students.

When the CoIn process is working well, it results in analysis of data that critiques practice and processes at all levels—classroom, departmental, and schoolwide. Applying the principles of action research within the conceptual framework of academic press, social

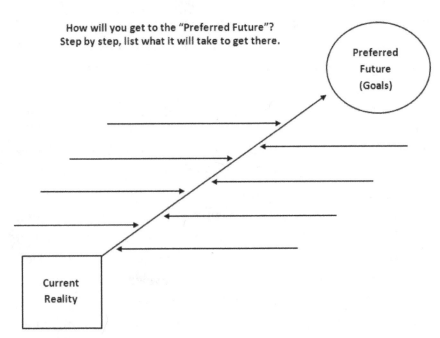

Figure 1.3 How to get to the preferred future. Source: Washington State OSPI

support, and relational trust allows the CoIn process to tu culture for learning in an intentional way.

Effective analysis of data and related actions leads to identification of best practice for *your* school. Action research initiates a dynamic relationship between change from the outside in, which starts at the schoolwide level, and change from the inside out, which starts at the classroom/department level. The findings of action research help foster a systems approach to change. This dynamic relationship between people's roles and levels of intervention will be further explored in parts II and III.

Action Steps—Moving CoIn to Action Research[2]

1. School leaders work to develop a school profile that consists of demographic, perceptual, contextual, and achievement data. Present the school profile to the entire staff. Ask each CoIn team to analyze the data through the lens of their grade level/content area. Keep it simple when reporting out. Do the evidence gathering and reporting yourself, rather than delegating it to others. Examples of analytics may include the following:

   a. Achievement data: Student growth, number of students passing classes at a C or better, number of students at standard
   b. Contextual: Types of programs that support student learning, including English language learning support, special education support, discipline data, community data/profiles
   c. Demographic: Socioeconomic, ethnicity, English language learners, attendance, dropout rate, school enrollment trends
   d. Perceptual: Climate, student and parent voice, engagement

2. Have each CoIn team analyze the schoolwide evidence and discuss the following:

   a. What does each of the different forms of data tell us about our schoolwide/department/grade-level/classroom practices?
   b. Focus on contextual evidence and discuss the following:

- What schoolwide/departmental/grade-level practices/programs do we have in place to support our outcomes?
- How are these programs meeting the following needs of our grade level/department:

  - Attendance,
  - Behavioral expectations/discipline referrals,
  - Social-emotional issues, and
  - Achievement?

- Focus on perceptual data—if there are existing climate surveys, discern the following:

  - Is there a high level of relational trust between groups?
  - Do students believe there is adequate support for their learning needs?
  - Do parents and students clearly understand the learning outcomes? Be aware that using perceptual, contextual, and demographic data wisely will positively affect achievement outcomes over time.

c. Based on those conversations, at the department level discuss how each form of evidence helped define the ideal in relation to the current reality, and then begin to formulate a department-level goal. This does *not* necessarily have to be a SMART goal.

- Based on the goal, identify systems of support within the department. What else might be needed?
- Identify outcomes of the goal—what will it look like to reach it?
- Agree on a way to keep score on progress toward the goals.
- Nuance the work by reviewing the other forms of data, such as contextual factors that might influence how you deliver

support. Remember—the most powerful data concerns the level of relational trust between groups.

3. While allowing teachers to find the answers to *their* research questions, be patient yet demanding, knowing that the answer will become clear as they learn within the process. Trust the CoIn process and the people who are doing the work.

SUMMARY:

When staff engage in action research to solve problems, they are more likely to take ownership of the work. The evidence they gather informs their practice and helps them make sense of the work.

OPPORTUNITY #6: ALIGNING CONTENT, INSTRUCTION, AND ASSESSMENT

Deep alignment is about looking very closely at the external standards by which students are assessed and making sure that the content that is taught matches closely with those standards so that students are able to achieve consistent measures of learning.

As teachers become more engaged with each other through the process of action research, it's important to bear in mind that what may be the best way to join forces is to ensure that what is being taught aligns with the measures by which students are being assessed. If teachers agree on the learning outcomes and how to measure them, they can develop meaningful ways to engage in teaching to best serve their students and then collaborate on common products, strategies, and assessments. Much has been written about the importance of alignment, yet it is overlooked in low-performing schools because implementing it requires that people work together, in the contexts of both grade levels and content areas.

Sometimes leaders and teachers believe that alignment has been accomplished by those who set the external standards, by those who write (or sell) the textbooks, or by those who create the district curriculum pacing guide. In accordance with the work of Schlegel and Salina (2015), we use the term *deep alignment* to refer to going beyond accepting prescribed standards and related curriculum in making sure that content correlates with externally prescribed standards and the related assessments.

The problem in schools is not instructional practice and/or related assessments and activities; rather, the problem is misalignment between content and assessment. Often in a low-performing school, alignment between what is learned and what is taught and tested is superficial at best. Deep alignment ensures that there is clarity between what is being taught and how the school is externally assessed. Teachers in a low-performing school are often left alone to make sense of *what* to teach, and the textbook or district materials *become* the curriculum and the assessment.

Often in low-performing schools, teachers rely on textbooks for their learning targets. The fact that textbook companies *claim* their content is aligned with external standards does not ensure that deep alignment is truly present. Reliance on textbooks robs teachers of the most important step: figuring out *what* to teach the students and collaborating on the *how*.

Insufficient knowledge regarding the standards combined with textbook dependency creates a situation in which instructional alignment can be only as deep as the textbook allows. Further, formal leaders in low-performing schools often run and hide from insisting that deep alignment take place. They fear the nature of the conversation that will result. The previous opportunities discussed will foster willingness to engage teachers in the deep alignment process.

Gavin Fulmer found in 2011 that regardless of context, teachers are more aligned with each other's practice than with expected learning outcomes as described by external standards. This version of group-think suggests that regardless of a school's location and demographics, educators are teaching lessons on similar content using similar materials and instructional methods.

Very often, the content teachers deliver and the state and/or national standards provided are not well aligned. Fulmer's data suggests that the level of alignment among teachers' instructional practice is greater than the level of content delivered in the state test—implying that *how we teach* is considered more important in the field than *what we teach*. Yet states, and now the Common Core, have spent millions of dollars in identifying the *what*.

Instructional practice at the building level has become a greater point of emphasis than the learning outcomes, for many reasons: (a) it is assumed that this alignment has already been done; (b) this is extremely difficult work; (c) instructional strategies are a much easier topic of conversation for leaders to broach with their teachers than alignment of content and standards; and (d) external consultants and professional development providers seem to offer patches, superficial bandages that are appealing to educators in need. These factors lead to a misunderstanding of what might be called "quick fixes" regarding student learning.

According to Schlegel and Salina's 2013 work, in low-performing schools, deep alignment combined with academic press, social support, and relational trust offered through schoolwide systems results in significant gains in student achievement, despite teachers making few or no changes in instructional practice.

The message here is *not* that instructional practice is not important. The message is that *aligned* instructional practice follows *after* relational trust has been built among teachers and deep alignment has been achieved.

When alignment between *what* we teach and *how* we assess is present, instructional practice will become a topic of conversation for the CoIn team members. It happens when they feel safe with each other and when they know they all have something to offer: clarity in terms of what they're teaching. Clarity provided by contextual, demographic, and perceptual data will inform pedagogical practice.

Supporting teachers in doing the heavy lifting of identifying outcomes requires time and patience. This work cannot initially be accomplished by having outside consultants provide support or other forms of personal development for low-performing schools. Leaders hoping that instructional practices will immediately be improved through the CoIn teams' process may be disappointed.

Initially, what will improve is not practice, but teachers' clarity regarding what they are teaching. Having increased clarity makes both teachers and students more goal driven, resulting in greater learning as measured by external assessments. After teachers learn to join forces using the principles of action research, they will quickly gain an understanding of what to teach. Then a space will open up for discussion of instructional practice.

Setting up the optimal conditions for learning makes good sense. Formal leaders do well to become familiar with how adult learners learn. This information will be invaluable for learning leaders as they work to create an environment and related strategies that support teachers who are engaged in the deep alignment process. As teachers learn to work together and make sense of *what* to teach and *how* to assess, district curriculum pacing will likely be better honored, and the textbook and the consultant become purposefully used resources rather than the drivers of change.

Along with allowing for the time and patience necessary for each person on the CoIn team to learn new behaviors that will foster new beliefs, leaders can also display visual representations of the work. Visuals make it easier to engage in the schoolwide shar-

ing of CoIn teams' products in a way that makes th̲. is
evident to colleagues and describes what each CoIn team ̲.
to be held accountable for. Leaders can offer a powerful visua
allows people to fill in what is missing, or what may or may not ̲.
implied by the picture.

Over time, people's understanding of the content represented by the visual will deepen and shift, becoming ever more complex. When teachers are willing to look at external standards in a way that deepens their understanding, Figure 1.4 may help them make sense of the work.

Use of this figure is described in the following Action Steps. A focus on alignment evokes important questions: Should content be valued above method? Do reform efforts emphasize instruction over subject matter? If the answer to the last question is yes, then it

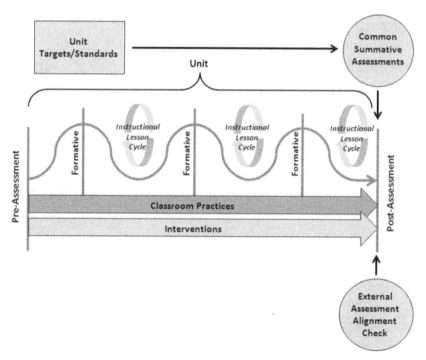

Figure 1.4 Curriculum, instruction, assessment (CIA) assessment framework. (Salina, Sylling, & Girtz, 2016).

critical that internal assessments be aligned with external assessments, and that the results gathered from internal assessments be used to inform instruction.

Action Steps for Aligning Content, Instruction, and Assessment

1. Provide each CoIn team with the content, instruction, and assessment framework. Have them articulate what the picture describes as it relates to their CoIn work. Prompts may include:

   a. Does the framework help your learning team identify a place to start?

   b. What action steps might you develop as a team to make this visual a living document you can use to jumpstart your work as a learning team?

2. During the process of deeply aligning learning targets with common formative and summative assessments that are aligned with external standards, engage in the following behaviors, many of which are advocated by Schlegel and Salina in their 2013 article:

   a. Develop a deep knowledge of the learning standards. This is essential.

   b. Build the capacity to identify and/or develop curricular materials that support the standards.

3. To promote the process of deep alignment within a CoIn team, use the following activities:

   a. Spend time immersed in the standard to develop common deep understanding.

   b. Continually revisit standards to make sure departmental knowledge is aligned.

   c. Write and share assessment items for individual standards, sharing student work samples during pilot efforts.

4. Implementing common formative assessment is where the magic begins. Weekly common formative assessments offer an opportunity for teachers to engage in discussions about student achievement. This process also develops relational trust as teachers rely on each other, taking turns in developing and sharing assessments.

5. Demonstrate, in words and actions, your belief in teachers and the process.

6. Continually point out that schoolwide systems are in place to support teachers and their students in achieving learning targets.

SUMMARY:

Achieving deep alignment between the curriculum and the external standards will help teachers know what to teach and help students to learn. Using visuals is an effective way to share, outline, and deepen understanding of this process.

OPPORTUNITY #7: BE PRODUCT DRIVEN

Effective leaders simultaneously create clear boundaries and allow the CoIn team autonomy to work within those boundaries. Then team members figure out what to expect from one another, and individual and group learning takes place when team members create products together.

The role of leaders in identifying organizational boundaries is not to control the conversation, but to allow CoIn members to come up with their *own* solutions within specific givens. If the approach taken by the formal leadership is a prescriptive one that says, "I need the CoIn process to unfold in this order and this is what it looks like," teachers will go through the process—but they won't necessarily buy into the work. That approach deprives teachers of the opportunity to make sense of the work and apply their new understandings to achieve their collective purpose statement.

This is not a linear model. The approach is messy and loosely coupled, but powerful leaders have faith that the teachers will be able to find common ground—especially when the stage has been set through an emphasis on clarity of purpose in, and the structure of, the CoIn team.

A useful analogy is that of a football field. The field's boundaries are clearly defined, and when people break the rules or step out of bounds, the referee throws the flag or blows the whistle; however, it's up to the team to move up and down the field within these constraints.

The first six opportunities are intended to help jumpstart the collaborative process; the trick is to ensure that it is sustained. As *behaviors* change as teachers learn how to collaborate, so will their *beliefs* in each other and in the importance of joining forces. The outcome will be a deepening of relational trust between team members and increased collective efficacy.

Providing equity regarding quality curriculum and instructional practices for each student is critical if the achievement gap is to be addressed, and it must be offered in a collaborative environment grounded in teaching and learning. When leaders ensure that each teacher is collectively engaged in identifying and implementing common essential learning outcomes, living their collective agreements, and embracing a sense of ownership regarding what should be taught, a culture for learning is established.

DuFour suggested that learning communities should be result driven. We find that using the term *product driven* (rather than *result driven*) is helpful in describing the work of a learning community in a low-performing school. The term is preferable because developing collective products is less intimidating for low-achieving schools than assessing whether they have achieved a specific result.

Coming to agreement on products such as a purpose statement, team norms, learning targets, formative and summative assessments, and curriculum pacing is a major triumph in a schoolhouse where few, if any, collective agreements have been honored. Further, these products help sustain the efforts to produce the results. It is not the results that drive the work; rather, results are outcomes of the product-driven efforts.

Often, becoming result driven reinforces the importance of writing SMART goals to specify areas in which to improve learning. SMART goals describe the desired results regarding student learning. Writing specific SMART goals before relational trust is developed and before deep alignment takes place in a low-performing school may actually result in distraction or a deep frustration, or, worse yet, a waste of time. In this case, creating SMART goals may not be wise.

Creating SMART goals in the CoIn process in a low-performing school may lead teachers who aren't used to joining forces into a conversation that is counterproductive. They may say that the previous teacher did not prepare them, or that parents are not involved in their child's learning. SMART goals describe, in specific terms, the outcome of their work; however, in a low-performing school, teachers already know that their students aren't learning and that the school is dysfunctional, so writing such a goal is a useless exercise that only reinforces the notion that student learning is outside of the teacher's span of control.

In fact, a SMART goal will most likely lead to dissatisfaction and increased isolationism as well as reinforce learned helplessness. For that reason, it's important to focus instead on the products, such as deeply aligned learning targets and common formative and summative assessments, as well as systems that support teachers and learning.

Even when the work is product driven, the leader does not control the outcome of the CoIn teams' work. Rather, the leader *insists that agreements be made and honored.* Thus, the fact that the work is product driven means that it's evaluated using evidence that can be used by the CoIn team that aligns with a common goal or outcome. We believe it is *understood* and that learning becomes a *byproduct* of living the conceptual framework and creating the related products that support that work.

Explicit products that CoIn teams create, implement, and celebrate constitute quick wins that build *relational trust.* Creating products together facilitates the development of a belief in success for everyone (*academic press*), and help is provided by teammates (*social support*) in achieving the desired outcome. Products can then be made public to everyone in the schoolhouse. The quality of the product is not the initial concern of the effective leader. Rather, the formal leader is concerned simply with whether products are being created and owned.

Critiquing rather than asking powerful questions often sends the message that staff missed something or got it wrong. Staff who feel powerless are not ready to hear those messages. What they want and need to hear is: "Wow, you did something together—good for you!" Staff are getting closer to success as long as the team is moving forward toward the desired goal. Over time, as teachers engage in deeper conversations that are focused on student learning and curriculum and instructional practices, they will also become more critical of their own work.

Recall that relational trust is created when people feel safe, know that both they and their colleagues having something to offer, and believe that others are willing to put in time to help. As products are developed and team members fulfill their collective purpose and live up to expected norms, staff become more likely to take risks—and over time, quality improves. Teachers will move from being product driven to being results driven and become more open to embracing differences to formulate new commitments to achieve their collective purpose.

The key to improvement efforts lies in leaders be   ᖀ
staff are capable of doing the work—just as leaders as
believe in their students. This shift from a reliance
defined standards to an alignment with internally understood.
gets is the magic that happens when the conceptual framework is in
place in a school—in other words, when academic press is coupled
with social support in a context of relational trust. Powerful leaders
have faith that teachers will make this shift, and they are patient as
they direct, guide, and support teachers in the CoIn process. Then
the focus is on learning for everyone—not just students.

Action Steps for Being Product Driven

1. Ensure that products are created for each goal that is developed through the action research process.

2. Develop a formal reporting system that requires each team to keep score on their ability to live up to each of the different agreements. Have each CoIn team report out to the entire staff on a monthly basis regarding the evidence (products) they have created.

3. Take note of agreed-upon expectations and provide specific feedback through one-on-one and small group conversations that recognize people for living up to agreements. Use the agreed-upon expectations as a diagnostic tool to remind people of their chosen goals.

4. Take time to celebrate successes.

SUMMARY:

Taking an intentional and methodical approach to creating products is likely to result in deeper awareness of school goals. Developing products as a team builds confidence and relational trust.

The seven opportunities for joining forces presented in part I are all about creating an environment of trust and contribution within a context of servant-leadership. When leaders initiate and model a top-down wave of personal accountability, a safe space is created for taking risks and implementing ideas.

By leading the way in dropping defenses, reengaging teachers with teachers, clarifying the work, declaring accountability to each other, making sense through action, aligning content and instruction, and being product driven, administrators prepare the ground for teachers to truly work together as colleagues in an atmosphere where each feels safe, has something to offer, and trusts that everyone will put in the time to move toward organizational goals.

NOTES

1. Available at http://catalogimages.wiley.com/images/db/pdf/9780787986186.excerpt.pdf.

2. Much of the material in the Action Steps for Opportunity #5 is grounded in the Washington State Office of Superintendent of Public Instruction's School Improvement Planning Process Guide, available at http://k12.wa.us/StudentAndSchoolSuccess/SIPGuide/SIPGuide.pdf.

II

The Success Team — Applying the Conceptual Framework

When adults and students in a school feel powerless, leaders must build a team that acts as champions for teachers and students. Such a group can be called a Success Team. The Success Team *monitors* student progress, *evaluates* the evidence, *connects* students to the school, and *implements* the components of the new counseling model. Part II describes how the team may form and take action.

The members of the Success Team can be counselors, specialists, psychologists, coaches, or assistant principals. Leaders can use people who are already in the building, reapportioning their time to allow them to connect teachers and students in ways that support students in the classroom. They can allow them to make a contribution to raising attendance, graduation rates, and grades as members of Collaborative Inquiry (CoIn) teams. The Success Team paradigm, and the members who comprise the team, must be adjusted to meet the needs and draw on the resources of each individual school.

Because school counselors/psychologists are the ideal personnel to implement the components of the new Success Team model, the process described below refers to the team members as counselors. However, readers are asked to keep in mind that any adult in the schoolhouse can be a part of the Success Team.

BEGINNING THE TURNAROUND

A school's powerless status does not reflect the dedication of its employees. At many struggling schools, counselors work hard to support students and increase the graduation rate. They try interventions that are used at most schools: sending letters to parents, making phone calls to students' homes, and having one-on-one conversations with teachers and students at crucial junctures. Sometimes, none of these measures seem to help.

What can leaders do to support Success Team members in their work of serving students and teachers? As has been noted, change starts with the all-important one-on-ones. Leaders can emphasize with counselors the importance of supporting and monitoring *all* students, *all* the time. Leaders can get buy-in from counselors by reminding them of their mission—of why they went into this work in the first place—and by listening carefully to their concerns. Leaders can also acknowledge their staff's expertise and act upon their suggestions.

At first, the counselors may fear that these changes are going to be just another fad they're supposed to embrace. School counselors have been through too many of those. The difference with this model is that instead of having someone else tell them what to do, they will be *asked* about what to do. They will be treated respectfully and asked for their input. This approach allows them to construct meaning for themselves.

Once counselors have been given a chance to construct their own meaning and relational trust has been built through leaders' genuine offers of support, they'll likely become willing to try new methods. Those methods may be based on recommendations from the 2012 American School Counselor Association (ASCA) National Model, which include:

- using data to identify goals
- serving as advocates for students and teachers

- increasing collaboration among stakeholders
- emphasizing accountability
- embracing systemic change.

The Success Team can form in an organic way. Members of the team, like those of each department in the high school, begin by developing their CoIn teams, in which they focus on how to operationalize the new model. Data, or evidence, is a big piece of the new puzzle. Evidence on graduation rates, course grades, attendance rates, and discipline referrals is used to help team members focus on the nature of their work.

The goals behind the Success Team, like those behind the other systemic efforts, are to suffuse the school with the conceptual framework: to create academic press, strengthen social support, and foster relational trust. Additionally, the Success Team works to redefine the role of the school counselor.

THE SUCCESS TEAM MEMBER'S ROLE

Too often, school counselors are relegated to administrative or disciplinary roles that do not allow these professionals to use their skills to the greatest advantage. The 2012 ASCA National Model recommends that school counselors spend time using data to *drive program development, implementation, and evaluation.* The model further suggests that counselors spend 80 percent of their time providing direct services, or working in the field. Finally, the model emphasizes four themes: advocacy, collaboration, leadership, and systemic change.

Redefining and shifting the roles of school counselors so that their program is in alignment with the most recent ASCA model is an important part of a turnaround program strategy. An effective leader will allow counselors to take on more leadership, and within that new role, to move toward the common goal of improving student achievement. Counselors realize this goal by monitoring and supporting students continuously through the application of academic press and social support in an atmosphere of relational trust.

Bear in mind that counselors and other Success Team members do not do all the "heavy lifting" of assisting students. Rather, they identify issues, advocate for students, connect students to systems, monitor progress, and evaluate the success of systems and programs designed to help students and teachers.

IMPLEMENTING THE SUCCESS TEAM

Leadership

One big change incorporated with the Success Team format is that formal leaders encourage team members to take leadership risks. Powerful leaders let team members know they can behave autonomously while fulfilling expectations that they will collaborate with each other and with administrators. As a result of these expectations, team members are likely to support each other as they advocate for *every* student, rather than focusing just on the ones who are in crisis. In this model, team members also use evidence and new academic programs to create systemic changes that move students toward graduation or other markers of achievement.

Before changes can be made effectively, relational trust must be built between the counselors and the administration—especially those leaders who supervise the Success Team. Through their behaviors, leaders can demonstrate their belief that counselors possess the skills to effect change. Administrators must trust Success Team members to identify and use their own gifts and skills in projects related to their own interests.

Once that trust has been established, team members feel free to devise systems to support students. As a counselor in a struggling school that implemented the Success Team model put it,

We experienced a change in viewing ourselves and our own abilities, and we were given the trust to try things, and we were given the rope to go ahead. The motto has been, "Just do *something*. Try something."

Leaders can do their part by making it safe for team members to test their ideas. They can also have members identify their areas of expertise and then allow tasks to be reassigned in a way that reflects their dispositions. Those who enjoy making home visits can go out into the community to meet with parents; those who are more interested in data analysis can collect and assess evidence.

The reality is that the counseling staff have relevant knowledge. Leaders can encourage them all to contribute, remembering that once people recognize where they fit and the part they play in the overall plan, they become excited about running with it.

Collaboration

Schools that are implementing a Success Team can't allow the staff to be disconnected from their colleagues. Powerful leaders emphasize collaboration as a tool and an expectation. Team members work with one another, with teachers, and with administrators. Most counselors will be relieved, because isolation is one of the biggest factors eroding their morale and contributing to the failure of interventions. If leaders make sure the collaboration is supportive, counselors are likely to try new things, fail at some of them, and still feel supported by the team.

Team members meet on a regular basis, mirroring the CoIn team format leaders implemented in academic departments. Leaders encourage team members to share information about students with each other more freely. They also support them in developing programs and processes centered on academic achievement, behavior management, and social-emotional needs that capitalize on their expertise.

ess Team model, every student is assigned a "guardian

ember of the Success Team who will check in two or three times a week to make sure the student is on track and that his or her learning needs are being met. Each counselor has no more than thirty to forty students to "shepherd." This may seem like a large number. If so, it will be necessary for team members to reprioritize their work, remembering that when teachers and students are present, it's important that team members be present with them.

Have team members repeatedly ask students three questions:

- Are you learning?
- Does your teacher like you?
- Do you get help when you need it?

These steps will improve communication. They also increase the support for students, who will begin to have a clearer understanding of what they'll have to do to graduate. Make sure every student knows who his or her "guardian angel" is.

Ask team members to be persistent in letting students know why they've been placed in a specific program, such as the after-school or the noontime tutorial program. Give them guidance in developing a program that allows them to act as advocates for students and teachers, with varying levels of intervention based on the students' individual needs.

As this program unfolds, it comes to resemble a triage or intervention model, with Level 1 being the lowest level of intervention and Level 3 representing the highest-need students. As advocates, school counselors can figure out what steps students need to take to graduate, tell the students what those steps are, and place students in whichever supportive programs will help them take those steps. During this process, it is essential that teachers be actively involved in the process and communicated with on a regular basis about th related action steps.

Systemic Change

The Success Team paradigm includes specific systems, such as one that implements and monitors evidence collection. Based on the available evidence, team members work with parents, teachers, administrators, and their CoIn team to connect all students with programs that accelerate learning through such efforts as homework tutoring, outside agency intervention, attendance/tardy support, and team meetings designed to support students in being successful.

The Success Team's effectiveness will be dependent on the level of support it receives from members of the leadership team, whose behavior ideally reflects that they care about meeting the team's chosen goals. These goals emerge through the team's CoIn process. Each of the members' collective goals is routinely brought to the leadership CoIn team, where the lead administrator of the relevant team shares the overarching goals, the expected outcome, and the evidence that will be relied upon to indicate success. Evidence that the school is moving closer to its goals may include increased attendance, a greater number of students passing classes, and fewer discipline/suspension referrals.

Once leaders have redefined the Success Team's role in a way that allows members to embrace autonomy, specialization, and collaboration, team members will be in a much stronger position to advocate for, and to model, three important elements: academic press, social support, and relational trust. Next we'll discuss how to implement all three within the context of the Success Team.

APPLYING ACADEMIC PRESS

Collecting and sharing evidence is the counselor's main way of creating academic press. Leaders do well to develop a user-friendly to provide weekly summaries of student performance, grade-level reporting of attendance, grades, suspensions, ...sions. Team members may want to track the evidence that ...ongly affects attendance and graduation rates. Time can be spent each week taking actions that the evidence indicates would help all schoolhouse employees meet their common goals.

Each week all team members receive a custom report, created by the administration, that tells them what percent of students are passing all classes, the attendance rates, and the number of discipline referrals. Ideally, the information will be disaggregated by school, department, and students. Additionally, constant examination of the evidence means that even in a larger school, learning support team members learn the students' names, allowing them to become more familiar with each child and his or her situation.

The next step is to create a simple color-coded system, applied to each student in the school, that is based on the evidence. Here's an example of such a system:

- *Red* means a student is missing credits, failing more than one class, and/or not meeting at least one state assessment standard.
- *Yellow* is assigned to students who have credits to make up but are making progress with credit retrieval and are following a graduation plan.
- *Orange* is the color for students who just need to pass a state assessment.
- *Green* is the color for students who are on track to graduate.

Once the system is in place, team members can work with students to write graduation contracts created to match each student's color-coded category. At this point, the data retrieval system serves two purposes: It identifies where students stand in the context of graduation, and it serves as a call to action that is likely to result in team members' connecting students to the resources and programs they need, both inside and outside the schoolhouse.

A system of categorization can become a key component of how team members monitor their caseloads. It's a good idea to send schoolwide and departmental evidence to administrators on Mondays, discuss the evidence at an administrative meeting on Tuesdays, and send it to all CoIn teams on Wednesdays. The academic evidence specifying what percent of students are passing all classes may be disaggregated by grade level and by department every week. A category that shows how many students have one or more F's is included in the evidence distributed to the administrators every Monday and provided at every CoIn meeting.

The evidence isn't just for the adults. It's smart to bring the kids into the loop too. At regular intervals (every other week seems to work well), leaders can share the information with the student council, and the council can report the attendance numbers to the whole school over the intercom every week. Another suggestion is to put up new posters in the halls each week that show the percentage of students in each color category.

The beauty of a good data system is that it's simple enough to allow everyone to understand and respond. The reports let team members see which departments might need more support, and they get teachers wondering how they can use the new information to help students in their classes. The reports also help leaders to know whether the systems they're using are working. Generally, the work of the Success Team's CoIn team begins with efforts to reduce the number of failing grades.

Team members may initially note grading fluctuations by academic term, especially if the school doesn't use a standards-based grading and reporting system. In the beginning, people can "game" the one hundred-point scale, and a pattern of low achievement may be apparent right up until the end of the report period—at which time grades spike. Those peaks and valleys will eventually begin to level out as teachers become clearer about the standards and align their teaching with them, and as students buy in to new support systems and get the help they need to more consistently achieve at high levels.

PROVIDING SOCIAL SUPPORT

The more accurate the evidence received by Success Team members, the better able they are to be intentional in providing systems that support student success. Team members who have been feeling powerless often realize that they need to offer more social support. A good first step for them is to start spending more time in the classrooms. In struggling schools, counselors will often call a student down to their office. In a school that is becoming powerful, counselors or other team members go into the classroom and talk with the student (and the teacher if necessary) there.

Team members using this system also start talking with the students about different things than they had previously. Rather than just reporting the student's status to the student, the member will offer support, including giving relevant information, which might include telling the student how to get a tutor, how to retrieve credits, and how to access resources related to state testing. The team members preserve privacy by talking with the students in a hallway or a quiet corner of the classroom. These conversations show both the teacher and the student that the team member is there to offer both of them support, another way of building relational trust.

Once teachers feel that the team members are on their side, they have more energy and incentive to support their students. If a student is struggling with a problem that is specific to him/her, a Support Team meeting (described further in part III) is held. The student is present, and relevant adults—parents or guardians, teachers, a counselor—will be there too. Then everybody comes up with ideas and input. Finally, they create an action plan. The team member monitors the plan by going into the classroom again if that is deemed most beneficial, and by keeping in touch with any outside agency that may be involved.

Another way of increasing social support is to strengthen leadership among students. Success Team members may choose to work with the math department to develop a mentorship program in which *all* students are challenged to find and use their own leadership talents. They may encourage students to mentor one another, particularly in math. Mentoring their peers gets students to have "skin in the game." It makes them more likely to encourage each other to come to school and to keep their grades up. In one school, students were calling each other from school on their cell phones and telling their friends to get out of bed and get to class!

Success Team members can also foster leadership by matching the student leadership team members with counseling students at the nearest college or university. The high schoolers and the college students meet at the university (an exciting experience for kids from a small town, many of whom have never seen a college campus), in groups and in pairs, to discuss personal responsibility and optimal choices. Then, when the high school kids go back to their school, they can do presentations for their schoolmates on those topics.

Team members can invite past graduates to come and speak at assemblies. The graduates can be asked to tell the students the steps they'll need to take if they're going to apply to college. The graduates can assure the high school students that they have to work hard and stay caught up on their schoolwork if they want to pursue higher education.

Under the Success Team system, members also partner effectively with parents. They make contact with them frequently and bring them in as partners invested in their child's education. "Come on over to the school tomorrow," team members may urge parents, whether it be to watch their child be in a music performance or do a presentation. Team members also call parents to rejoice with them when a student succeeds; such measures show students that multiple adults are invested in their achievements and make the school feel more like a family. More information about the role of the parent is provided at the end of part III.

Finally, team members can improve social support through specific programs. For example, staff at one low-achieving school created a twenty-minute tutorial session that students attended during lunch period. Team members can also figure out which academic and/or social support systems (such as credit retrieval and state testing assistance) are most appropriate for particular students.

BUILDING RELATIONAL TRUST

Boosting the level of relational trust in the schoolhouse begins when Success Team members become visible and present. They do so by talking one-on-one with teachers, listening to their ideas about types of support that would improve teaching and learning. The next step is to integrate teachers' thinking into viable programs grounded in academic achievement, improved behavior, and attention paid to social-emotional needs. The more teachers receive support in helping students succeed through academic achievement and social support systems, the more likely it is that they'll reconnect with students and offer them assistance.

Success Team members can further develop relational trust by reaching out to parents and letting them know (a) where their children stand academically and (b) what resources are available to them.

Evidence gathered through the Success Team can also be used to create relational trust. Data can be used in two different ways: as grounds for punishment, or as a starting point for growth. If changes are going to be made successfully, people have to feel safe, and data needs to be seen as information that informs work rather than as a consequence of poor teaching that justifies punishment.

Team members can build a safe environment for one another by doing three things more intentionally:

• listening,
• devoting more time to each other, and
• incorporating each other's ideas.

Making these changes is likely to bond the team members into a cohesive unit. As one team member in a school that made it a goal to implement these measures put it, "We are not an island. We cannot close our doors. We have the same purpose." Success Team members in schools that are becoming powerful see themselves as dependent on and accountable to each other—the definition of relational trust. As they move toward their goals, they can keep learning within this safe context.

LESSONS FROM THE SUCCESS TEAM

To discern the results of using this comprehensive counseling system, schools can use historical evidence, such as graduation rates and academic achievement, gleaned from state and school records. They must pay attention to social-emotional needs such as teen pregnancy, suicide, gang violence, and other context-specific issues. They can also conduct semi-structured interviews with survey and focus groups to get perceptual evidence.

Subjective reports generally support the "hard" evidence. Teachers in one school that had built and incorporated a Success Team reported that as their trust in their colleagues, counselors, and administrators grew, their effectiveness increased, and so did their belief in their fellow teachers' effectiveness. They also noted that they felt more confident in their work and that they believed the administration had their backs.

According to the surveys from one school, teachers in a schoolhouse that has incorporated a Success Team have the three things that people must possess if relational trust is to grow: a feeling of emotional safety, the belief that everyone has something to offer, and the sense that the time and effort that are needed for success will be invested.

At schools where these three elements were present, students often report having a new belief that teachers care about them and are willing to help them. Both students and teachers indicate that their feelings of anonymity have decreased. Teachers and learning support team members embrace a focus on making sure every student is known. Furthermore, they demonstrate care for all students and *show* that they expected them to succeed.

Having greater access to and time with administrators increases teachers' sense that they are cared for, and having greater access to and time with teachers makes students feel cared for. Relational trust grows after administrators and counselors show respect for and interest in each other, in teachers, and in students *as individuals*. Furthermore, when students realize that data will be used to support rather than to punish them, their trust in their school grows.

COUNSELORS' PERCEPTIONS

Counselors who feel powerless often report that they operate largely in isolation and in crisis mode. Because these counselors are so busy putting out fires, the kids who aren't "burning" don't get much attention. Struggling schools often put one counselor in charge of seniors, meaning that counselor is likely to be overwhelmed and is unlikely to have time to attend to the caseload satisfactorily. Dividing up the seniors among counselors, improving the collaboration among counselors, and imposing the Success Team's color-coding and data analysis systems makes a huge difference for these counselors. Then their job feels much more manageable.

Again, counselors can do their jobs more effectively and with a greater sense of meaning if they spend more time out in the field, going to classrooms to talk with students and teachers and being more visible and available. Doing so allows them to get to know the students as individuals, which results in greater respect for both parties. Efficient use of evidence allows counselors to know what's going on with any student at any time, to share that information with their colleagues, and to intervene in a timely fashion.

Counselors who engage in these behaviors arenM M t just putting out fires. They are also tending to the students who are succeeding, helping them to focus on getting to college. Attending to *all* students not only raises achievement levels, but also improves counselors' morale and sense of efficacy. Counselors in schools that implement the kind of system described here tend to report feeling more powerful, more satisfied, and more productive.

TEACHERS' PERCEPTIONS

In schools where a large percentage of the students are behind academically before the new Success Team model is put in place, teachers feel overloaded and operate in crisis management mode. Once they start receiving additional support from Success Team members and administrators, they have new options. They can do the following:

- Try different teaching innovations without fearing that, if it doesn't work, the repercussions will be severe.
- Connect more with their students as individuals.
- Gain a stronger sense of their own efficacy in an atmosphere of relational trust.

A teacher at a school that uses a Success Team format said that the model offers "an early spotlight and consistency" that helps students, team members, and teachers relax into faith in the system and one another. Teachers at such a school are likely to see the commitment that counselors are demonstrating through the Success Team and to appreciate the organization brought about through the use of evidence and the student categorization system. Thus, the model begins to affect the pedagogical system.

STUDENTS' PERCEPTIONS

Students in schools that have a Success Team say they feel more cohesive as a student body. They're more likely to work together to get attendance rates up and keep the school clean in efforts to earn the resulting privileges. Their school spirit grows noticeably. Also, as they feel increasingly cared for by counselors and teachers, they extend that caring to one another.

Leaders may be surprised by the extent to which students in schools that are becoming powerful tune in to the data. They see it as an indication of concern and as part of an effort on the part of the teachers and the Success Team members to support them. As one student said, "I know exactly what I have to do. We can't really get away with stuff or hide." Another student agreed, saying, "They call your parents and let them know [your academic status] way more often now than before."

Students are also likely to support making data public, allowing them to demonstrate concern for one another. Students may share their grade or graduation status with each other and ask each other for help when they need it.

Openness with the evidence appeals to students for two reasons:

- It makes them feel better informed and helps give an overview of what they need to accomplish.
- It makes them feel, correctly, that the adults in their lives have the same information about them and are sharing it in efforts to help them.

Additionally, when evidence is gathered and made transparent, students are more likely to ask for help in applying to colleges and making postsecondary decisions. They appreciate the help of adults in their lives in using data proactively. As one student put it, "The counselor is like a big brother to help you out and keep you on track." In short, when students understand that evidence is being gathered and disseminated in efforts to support them, they feel cared for.

IMPACT OF THE SUCCESS TEAM MODEL ON THE SCHOOLHOUSE

The increase in academic press, social support, and relational trust supplied by the Success Team is likely to produce newfound academic success, which has schoolwide implications.

An increase in pass rates means that online credit retrieval is used less often; as a result, the district saves considerable money, and the need for academic intervention programs is reduced, which frees up teachers for the academic core. Moreover, an increased course pass rate means that fewer students have to repeat classes. In addition to providing the opportunity to reassign teachers, the cost savings means students have access to more electives, additional Advanced Placement classes, and College in the High School courses. These changes are highly beneficial in a low-income school.

WHAT TO WATCH FOR

Staff at schools that incorporate a Success Team often feel buoyed as a result of their new success. At the same time, they are likely to be tired. They are putting in new efforts in new ways. Leaders have a responsibility to be protective and supportive of their staff's resources.

The increased sense of teamwork in a school that is moving from powerless to powerful is one of the main supports that leaders can build on. Team members succeed when they build relationships with each other, with teachers, with parents, and with students. The Success Team gives everyone involved several ways to build those relationships, and leaders do well to nurture and celebrate them.

WHAT THE MODEL MEANS FOR TEAM MEMBERS

The Success Team counseling model was created for and first implemented in a particular low-achieving school, and it was in that school that its effectiveness was first demonstrated. But the principles the model is founded on are universal, and any school can benefit from the Success Team model, especially if it's based on the principles of the conceptual framework. Additionally, the model must include a methodical way to record, analyze, and act on the evidence.

The toughest—and most important—part of putting the model in place is probably changing the way Success Team members think about their jobs. If administrators want to see that change, they have to encourage team members to take leadership roles and to collaborate with them, with their colleagues, and with teachers to improve academic achievement in the schoolhouse.

The first step leaders can take in making that change is to model relational trust by behaving in a trustworthy way. They can employ principles of servant-leadership, emphasizing characteristics described by Larry Spears in 2000—listening, community building, and the growth of people—to empower others. A model based on relational trust is most likely to succeed when administrators and Success Team members jointly understand that the team members are both the beating pulse of the school and the conduit through which information flows: to students, to teachers, and to parents.

The transformation in a schoolhouse starts with people feeling connected to one another. That connection grows when people are respected and known as individuals. It's easy to reduce a student to one or more labels, but that's no way to serve the student.

Success Team members at one school were working with a student who was failing many classes and was known as a "gangbanger." Once they began to know this student by name and context rather than by reputation, the team members saw that other labels could apply as well. The student was highly intelligent and, despite being only seventeen, a devoted father to his young daughter. Team members encouraged him to think of how his future would affect her future, and he made the decision to graduate.

The student stopped doing drugs, stayed away from the gang, and worked hard and successfully to make up classes he had failed. Soon the student's only barrier to graduation was the state high stakes test. The night before the exam, the student chose to disregard the restraining order against him in an attempt to see his daughter. His daughter's mother called the police, who arrested the student and took him to the station.

At that point the student begged the police officers, "Please, can you get me processed in time to get to school tomorrow morning? This is my last chance to pass the test!" The startled officers, who knew this student as a tough kid who didn't care about school, complied, and when the student made it to school the next morning in time to take the Hispie (which he passed), many of the team members had tears in their eyes. Their change of attitude *toward* the student had resulted in a change of attitude *in* the student that may have lifelong effects. That's the kind of transformation that makes most educators go into the schoolhouse in the first place.

When the adults in a schoolhouse care for all students and expect them to graduate, and when they align the work of the Success Team with a conceptual framework that is grounded in servant-leadership—that's when the tools become available to increase academic achievement.

Success Team members can apply academic press by using evidence to track and communicate to students the belief that they can do what they must to graduate. They can demonstrate social support by offering students programs that will help them succeed, and work to make sure they take advantage of those programs. When academic press and relational support have become an integral part of the school, relational trust blooms. Here are some strategies team members can use to let staff and students know that academic press and social support are present:

1. Develop a *simple* monitoring system that tracks every student's progress toward graduation. This system includes real-time evidence regarding each student's status, including grades, credits, disciplinary measures taken, attendance, and mandatory tests.

2. Communicate, communicate, and communicate some more. Instead of remaining in your office, be out and about throughout the day—in classrooms, hallways, and the cafeteria. Talk with identified students and teachers on a regular basis—up to three times a week.

3. Engage in these conversations with three purposes in mind: to let the student know that you're paying attention to his or her progress toward graduation; as proof that you believe in the student's ability to succeed; and to make sure that the student feels like a part of the school family and is receiving (and attending) the necessary school and/or community services.

4. Be seen as advocates for teachers. Everyone knows that teachers play an essential role in the process of moving all students toward achievement and graduation. Teachers want their students to succeed, so let them know about the available support systems and ask them how you can help them to

help their students. Listen to what they have to say, and plug their suggestions into the plan of action for the students.

5. Take your CoIn teamwork seriously. Bounce successes and failures off of your colleagues. Help to build common language, goals, and a culture for learning. Remember, when everyone shares the same goal, knows what the current status is, knows what part to play, and uses common language to describe it, everyone feels accountable. Model that accountability.

When leaders encourage Success Team members to use these strategies, relationships will develop. Within these relationships, team members can learn each student's name and offer *each student* academic press and social support. No longer represented as empty data, students become living beings with particular gifts, goals, and contexts.

At the same time, increasing the level of collaboration among Success Team members enables them to have greater efficacy, especially when they commit to supporting teachers and their work. When adults model supportive behavior, students pick it up too. Finally, the team members have the responsibility to redefine their roles, recognizing that they bear responsibility for students' academic performance. When the Success Team really pays attention to students' academic lives, students feel connected to the school and start fulfilling team members' expectations that they will succeed.

III

Schoolwide Systems—Putting It All Together

Creating change from the outside in requires building relational trust at the organizational level. One way to build and support this trust is to implement schoolwide systems to support teaching and learning rather than relying on fragmented individual efforts. Especially in a school that is struggling, systems can and must be built to support behavior management, social-emotional learning, and academic achievement.

Many schools address those three areas through a variety of programs and activity-driven efforts that are disconnected. Schools in the process of becoming powerful move toward a more ideal reality by implementing integrated systems that align with the conceptual framework of academic press, social support, and relational trust.

Part III describes how systems were developed and managed at one particular school. Although system creation and implementation will have to be tailored to each individual school, examining this case study can help inspire leaders to see that the resources for school change are already in the schoolhouse. Building schoolwide systems begins the process of connecting the teachers, students, and parents to the school; developing positive relationships among staff, students, and leaders; and allowing staff and students to envision their future.

When schoolwide systems and department/grade-level needs are aligned in supporting the behavioral, academic, and social-emotional needs of students, then rapid change will take place in the classrooms because individual teachers will see the collective whole working together to support their efforts. Figure 3.1, similar to one in *Powerless to Powerful: Leadership for School Change*, is offered here to illustrate this change process.

Creating change from the outside in requires building relational trust at the organizational level. Please note that while this book is focused on school change, district systems must also support the nature of the work if it is to be sustainable. Special education and career and technical programs must be included, for they are critical in the collaborative process that is integrated to support department/grade-level and classroom changes.

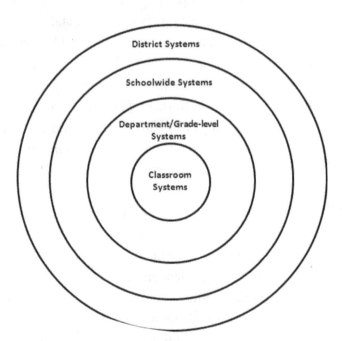

Figure 3.1 Interdependence of systems.

Especially in a school that is struggling, systems can and must be built to support behavior management, social-emotional learning, and academic achievement. These systems are grounded in the principles found in the conceptual framework (Figure 3.2).

Recognize that regardless of the nature of the systems being implemented, whether designed to improve student behavior or student learning, specific supports need to be in place (*social support*). Additionally, high expectations coupled with a belief that each student can achieve the desired results (*academic press*) needs to be in place in a safe environment where support is offered to achieve the goal (*relational trust*).

When this happened at the school under discussion, administrators and educators saw a shift in their levels of support. Their initial reality was the opposite of the ideal breakdown of leveled services, as seen below. After three years of systemic development, the triangle of interventions had become inverted and resembled the ideal.

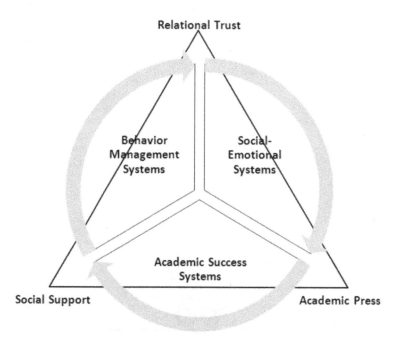

Figure 3.2 Alignment of systems with conceptual framework.

Programs at each level, which are described later in this section, included those in Figure 3.3.

This is where things get dangerous, for a couple of reasons. This section describes some of the actions leaders may take as they do their work. But it is important to note that things become more complicated in the implementation stage. This part of the book takes a complex, integrated system—one of interdependence and interactions—and displays it as simply a collection of simultaneously working parts.

Sometimes it's necessary to break down an organically moving system into discrete parts to conceptualize the work, but doing so creates the possibility of failing to acknowledge the very nature of how things actually function. When people lose sight of the complex interactions between parts in a system and look only at the categorized pieces within the system, their understanding may be

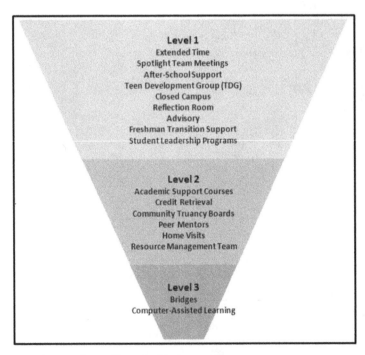

Figure 3.3 Examples of leveled interventions.

oversimplified—and that can be dangerous. However, simplification is sometimes necessary, and even preferable, to facilitate initial understanding of complex issues or processes.

Delineating work requires the creation of a series of steps that often become disjointed and play out as independent activities. Work focused on discrete programs in a schoolhouse is often driven by activities instead of by organizational goals. Leaders, teachers, students, and parents become slaves to the activities rather than being the architects of the goals of the school.

Integrated work is driven by clear principles that are interdependent—often easy to conceptualize but extremely hard to actualize. However, the results are transformational.

Leaders in high-pressure scenarios might prefer to turn to this section in hopes of finding a checklist of potential interventions to "fix" things. (The answers usually *are* in the back.) However, that kind of process would dismiss the entire message of this and the first *Powerless to Powerful* book, and likely produce results similar to those of the last several decades of education reforms.

As a busy leader, you don't have time for that. "But the process described in this book seems slow and eternal," you might protest. That's not necessarily so. The school used as an example here had good results in one year, and fantastic results in three. Over time, the results simply get stronger. This is why the saying "Slower is faster" makes sense. Students are short-timers, but leaders are playing the long game. A school's leadership needs to serve students both *now*, and *for years to come*.

Therefore, the next section details types of programs and interventions that relate to the principles of the conceptual framework as a way for leaders to organize their work. As you read, you may think, "We already have a program like that," and likely you do! Few of these programs are new or unique. It is the *system of organization and application* that actualizes the programmatic effects.

The system helps to make the thinking behind the actions visible. As leaders make their thinking visible, the spirit behind the interventions becomes apparent and actually becomes a part of the work as well. As a nimble and supportive system develops, educators increasingly respond positively when new mandates come down the line.

You know what it looks like when new mandates are passed down in a powerless school. Just when you get comfortable with something, the state adds requirements, changes the rules, or throws some new curveball your way. "Here they go again" is a common refrain in schools.

At the school described here, instead of using that refrain as fuel for learned helplessness or impetus for disengagement based on feelings of powerlessness, educators responded to change with a greater calm. Fear responses lessened, and change simply became a natural, expected part of the culture of education. Why? Because now the leaders and staff had systems that could handle new inputs and respond productively to support all stakeholders.

One leadership team member said, "Whatever they throw at us is okay, because we have a process. The process doesn't change. Bring it on!" Having a stable process in place meant educators could accommodate productive change.

As the leadership Collaborative Inquiry (CoIn) team worked to meet students' needs, they paid particular attention to themes that repeatedly emerged during one-on-ones and in reviews of the forty-five-day plan. Interventions were developed only after much conversation, and they were implemented with great intentionality. The team intended to build support systems for any student who needed them, and, they maintained, "they *all* need them." As you read, consider what programs are already in existence in your school and how they might fit within the framework described below.

In making the process visible, the team aligned the development of systems with the three levels of intervention. Conceptualized as levels of intervention (Figure 3.3), when the work began, more than 80 percent of students were in Level 3. Several years later, less than 3 percent were.

Implementing the work effectively flipped the triangle and allowed the school to align resources in a way that honored more students' needs rather than disproportionately funding emergency Level 3 interventions. The interventions within the three levels are described below based on the area they were primarily designed to influence: academic achievement, behavioral management, or social-emotional. Bear in mind that categorization is an oversimplification intended to foster clarity and understanding. Of course no particular effort has only a single impact or applies to just one category.

The leadership team developed Level 1 systems by asking, "How do we keep all student statuses 'green'?"—all the while knowing the levels aren't static: Students may be "green" in one content area and not in another, attendance fluctuates, and needs change. All students are served by Level 1 systems in some way, and some may require other levels as well. Although interventions cut across purposes, they are categorized below by their main target for improvement.

LEVEL 1 SYSTEMS

In a low-performing school, *all* students are struggling and will require a host of systems. These schools often are overwhelmed by the number of students who are failing academically, socially-emotionally, or behaviorally, and all of the ideal "greens" are likely "reds" to begin with; the triangle is inverted. *When that many students are struggling, colors don't really matter—action does.* Actions are required to address students' needs in the realms of aca-

:ess, social support, and behavior management. It's only as
; are implemented and students begin to change status that
start to be meaningful.

Again, color doesn't really matter initially; yet it's important
that students be aware of and understand their statuses. They also
need to feel supported in changing their statuses, and to know that
teachers, counselors, and administrators believe they can raise their
achievement level.

When half of the students in a school are not on track to graduate, a host of interventions across needs is required. Examples are
offered in Figure 3.4.

When all students have "red" status, adults in the school can't
tend to each one at the level needed. However, they can look for
emergent themes based on need to begin the work. Creating and
implementing responses to these themes is messy and nonlinear.
Initial efforts feel more like stopping the bleeding than making
progress. Eventually a more rigorous approach can be intentionally

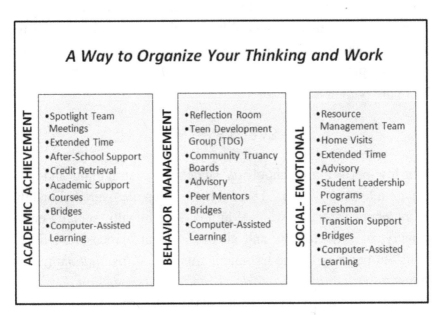

Figure 3.4 Schoolwide systems.

applied, using a lens of action research to determine appropriate interventions.

At all times, those in the schoolhouse must align their beliefs and behaviors with the conceptual framework, or efforts will be a repeated cycle of fractured, sporadic attempts that leave people feeling burned out and powerless. Disjointed attempts won't move the system forward.

So where do you start? It almost doesn't matter. Review student needs and tend to them in groups rather than individually in the beginning. Some of the programs you develop will likely resemble the examples offered below, informed by a school that successfully implemented the turnaround process.

Academic Achievement

Extended Time

One intervention was named Extended Time (ET) to denote the notion of extended learning opportunities within the school day and to indicate that teachers were prepared to invest additional time to help students succeed. Instead of an add-on beyond the school day,

Level 1 Systems

Academic Achievement	Behavior Management	Social-Emotional
Extended Time	Teen Development Group (TDG)	Advisory
Spotlight Team Meetings	Closed Campus	Freshman Transition Support
After-School Support	Reflection Room	Student Leadership Programs

Figure 3.5 Examples of Level 1 interventions.

ET became an embedded, intentional time that all students and staff engaged in, another effort to emphasize the "we" in the "together we will" effort.

ET required reconfiguration of the school day schedule for everyone. It consisted of twenty minutes attached to third period. While students with all grades of C+ and better went to a fifty-minute lunch (or other opportunities described later), students who had C's or below attended twenty minutes of additional support time in the content area(s) of need. Academic press was on: Students were expected to be above average.

Originally, students might stay in their third-period classes and get extra time and support from their teacher in that class. But as ET evolved, if students struggled in other content areas, teachers would call each other and say that a student would be on the way. What started as a study hall became a more intentional support time.

Administrators kept track of overall grade results with a data dashboard and constantly asked: "Is the data current?" Since the system was based on course grades, it was imperative that grades be reported in a timely and accurate manner. Kids began to press teachers to ensure that grades were up-to-date. The administrative team never had to ask teachers to do that, because the kids were on it! Academic press evolved. No longer just teacher-to-student, it was now student-to-teacher as well. The onus was on teachers to be accountable to students, and students were compelled to pay attention to how they were doing in the classroom.

A shift took place. Before ET was implemented, if a student needed help, he or she had to seek it out independently of systemic assistance. ET sent the message that students were worth time dedicated to support them and that helping them was part of teachers' work. ET was the first schoolwide system in which students could ask for help.

After some time had passed and fewer students were failing classes, the administrative team sought answers. They asked the student council what was going on, and the students replied that the teachers cared and that teacher caring made the difference.

Teachers were asked the same question in a staff meeting. They commented on how nice it was that students finally cared, and that student caring made the difference. Teachers now heard students asking how to be above average (to meet the C+ requirement) and perceived that concern as care. When students received help from teachers, they perceived that assistance as care.

Of course, the reality is that everyone cared before ET was implemented—and these were the same teachers and students. ET was just the first system to bring the perception of care to the fore and support it.

Students began to understand that ET had been created to help them be successful, and that teachers believed success was possible for them. Kids expressed appreciation for the relational trust that this program fostered; they liked knowing that they were safe, that teachers had something to offer them, and that help was available.

Sometimes they needed a lot of help. Teachers began to assist students with goal setting, especially when they had three or more F's, which felt overwhelming to students. This process helped students to envision their futures at the same time that it made the work manageable and goals attainable.

Students who met the C+ benchmark had other options while their classmates were in ET. Freshmen and sophomores could take a longer lunch. Juniors and seniors, too, could use the time for extended lunch, but also had the opportunity to earn an open campus. That privilege was earned by meeting several goals concerning grades, school cleanliness, character as demonstrated by particular behaviors, and attendance rates. Athletes who had away games could use the time to take tests and do makeup work. Clubs held their meetings during ET, and leadership students led events like karaoke.

ET continues to evolve at the school under discussion. Educators note that the school grade data shows peaks and valleys that are predictable around reporting and conferencing periods, especially given that the grading systems continue to rely on the one hundred-point scale. It would be interesting to see the impact of a shift to a standards-based grading and reporting system, but the current system provides timely support in attempts to intervene before student deficits become overwhelming.

Spotlight Team Meetings

Too often, parents aren't involved in the school in a systemic way. Including them in Spotlight Team meetings is a way to connect them to the school at Level 1. Any teacher from any grade can call a time-out for a student who is perceived to be academically (or socially/emotionally) declining or in jeopardy. The counselor is then contacted, and relevant partners are engaged to help develop a support plan for the student. (This is another instance in which the Success Team is so important, because the team members can see results from more than one class and look for patterns.)

After the grade-level counselor collects more evidence and interacts with the student and teachers, the parent is included and the focus shifts to systems of support. But before a parent is ever brought in, the school needs to have something to offer; if parents don't feel that they have options or are being heard, stagnant one-way communication may result.

When a parent comes in and is listened to, has choices, and is offered multiple levels of support from the school, relational trust is likely to develop, and parents are likely to become a part of the solution. It is important that the parent see the teacher at the table. It's not a good idea to circumvent the teachers and invite only the counselor and the parent. This Spotlight Team meeting is important for the teachers as well. They need to see that they're not alone, that an entire team is developing a plan that they'll implement together to move toward a common goal.

After-School Support

The school provided a non-optional extended learning opportunity for students who were falling behind in their schoolwork. This system was designed for any student getting an F in any class. Teachers checked grades on a weekly basis to make sure the right students were attending. Administrators noticed the most positive effects when teachers took action by having students take specific steps on the same day, rather than providing longer-ranging support strategies or passive study hall opportunities. Teacher engagement was crucial.

Behavior Management

Teen Development Group

During ET and lunch, students who were struggling to get to school on time—or at all—came to Teen Development Group (TDG) to work on building relationships and envisioning their future. Facilitated by a staff member, TDG brought in outside role models and community mentors, supported personal goal setting, and implemented a variety of programs, such as character education plans that promote resilience education, particularly for students with behavior disorders or learning disabilities.

Students needed 90 percent attendance over two weeks to show evidence of a new behavior and get permission to leave the group. Requiring students to demonstrate a new, desired behavior and then rewarding them for it is key to the effectiveness of this intervention. Supporting the new behavior also gives Success Team members the access and ability to connect students to other systems based on needs that emerge as staff listen to the students while they all eat lunch together.

The barriers to attendance usually had nothing to do with the students not wanting to be there. Often students were late or absent because they had to babysit younger brothers or sisters, didn't have an alarm clock, had to walk too far, or had home lives that were not supportive of their getting to school. Once factors over which the school could exercise some control were tended to with extra support, students no longer had excuses for not showing up. TDG students' attendance rates rose dramatically.

Closed Campus

Initially the whole campus was closed, but then formal leaders decided to divide lunch into two periods, separated by grade levels: grades 9 and 10 ate at the same time, as did grades 11 and 12. Freshmen and sophomores had to stay on campus, but juniors and seniors could earn an open campus. They were allowed to leave campus for lunch if (a) their grades were an average of C+ or better; (b) as a class they achieved 95 percent attendance; and (c) they demonstrated good character—which included keeping the school clean and responding appropriately to student altercations.

When the effort began, custodial staff thought of cleaning graffiti off school grounds as a normal part of their workload. After leaders implemented the new system, that part of the custodians' work was largely eliminated—graffiti was rarely seen.

Reflection Room

Originally piloted with special education students, the Reflection Room later opened up to other departments. When a behavior issue arose, a teacher would prompt the student to think deeply about the issue; the student would be given time and space to go reflect on the behavior that caused the issue. The time of reflection could be as short as one period of the day, depending on the issue and the student's response to it.

Because the school supported restorative justice, the student wrote reflective thoughts and then went back to attend to the trust that had been damaged, working to repair the relationship. Ideally, students in the Reflection Room would reflect before they acted. Sometimes teachers heard a new perspective from students, and both were able to be more open and vulnerable.

Social-Emotional

Advisory

Grade-level advisories were developed to pursue notions concerning character, respect, courtesy, citizenship, and other characteristics. The district added the traits to its calendar, and all schools worked to honor the intent of developing the characteristics in their students. Community members helped develop the program, and together stakeholders described what it meant to be a member of the school. When students demonstrated a particular quality, they were acknowledged with a bracelet inscribed with that quality.

Representatives from each advisory went to leadership meetings to discuss common issues and help develop lessons. For example, when cell phones became an issue in the classroom, the advisory courses responded with a lesson that taught how to deal with a request to put cell phones away.

Advisory plays an important role as a communication tool. It allows schoolwide behavioral expectations to be shared. Additionally, it provides an opportunity to offer social-emotional support.

Because students in each advisory period are organized as a cohort, they have the same teacher for all four years. Each teacher's student profiles are intentionally split across red/yellow/green statuses so that no single teacher has a disproportionate load. Advisory is where students learn to understand rather than fear their status.

They also learn about the variety of levels of support available to them. Formal leaders communicate the *what* and the *whys* of the support system to the students. "We think they know about all this available support; they don't," acknowledged one administrator. For example, with freshmen, since there are no state tests to influence status, each student is classified as only green (all passing grades) or red (one or more F's). Advisory teaches students about the classification system and how to successfully change their status.

Each year gets more nuanced, with extra requirements, and advisory helps to make the systems transparent and accessible. Additionally, it facilitates peer support for students as they pursue a green status. Teachers get dedicated time without a predefined curriculum to listen to students' stories and strengthen relationships. Before advisories existed, an external inventory asked students if they had an adult in the building whom they trusted; 48 percent said yes. After advisory was introduced, that number shot up.

Freshman Transition Support

Administrators and counselors met with 8th graders to introduce themselves and share information regarding graduation and changes at the high school. Transition Plans were created with counselors and key staff at both buildings, who met to identify specific student needs—English language learners (ELL), Special Education, honors, Bridges (described later), attendance, behavior, and so forth—to ensure that supports were in place for students as they moved to the high school.

High school visitations were conducted in May so that students could see their classrooms and participate in a Moving Up assembly. The administration offered a parent information night to converse and offer facts about the high school experience, elective courses, and graduation. It was standing room only; the school had never seen such a large parent turnout for a discussion related to academics and graduation.

The more the high school communicated, the more its systems were considered across the district. The middle school adopted the red/yellow/green designations to promote consistency across schools. As a result, when red-status 8th graders visited the high school in March, they were better able to envision their future.

The greatest depth of programming is available in Level 1, as that is where the bulk of students are—or, at least, they will be eventually as the intervention triangle is reoriented once aligned interventions are offered. Levels 2 and 3 have more focused interventions that are brought into play only when Level 1 interventions aren't enough.

Student Leadership Programs

The leadership program was reformed based on the three goals of connecting to the school, envisioning the future, and building relationships. The course had three levels. Freshmen and sophomores took a content-focused leadership course. A traditional associated student body leadership course was also offered that created schoolwide activities supporting the three goals. One example is students helping to develop the criteria they had to meet to earn the open campus. The nontraditional class, which was co-taught, centered on the three goals, both for the school and for the individuals in the class.

Students applied to be a part of the class, were recommended by teachers, or were considered a priority for inclusion due to their participation in the migrant program. The course typically had a very diverse profile. In the future, the student leadership program will also include a self-contained leadership class for high-needs students that will help connect them to the school.

Assemblies or class competitions developed by the associated student body leadership were built on the three goals. The grades and attendance of each class counted in the competitions. One year at the homecoming assembly, students celebrated their graduation rate and, according to one administrator, "The kids went nuts!" He continued, "We showed them our data versus the state's. Now attendance skyrockets on assembly days. Kids just go; we don't even have to ring a bell."

LEVEL 2 SYSTEMS

Academic Achievement

The intent of Level 2 academic systems is to prepare students to successfully meet state testing mandates. Instead of sending students who are exhibiting behavioral or academic problems to the teacher, thereby isolating both student and teacher, powerful leaders create multiple systems that kick in simultaneously to support both educators and kids.

Leaders can help everyone be invested by removing barriers. For example, when teachers say students have to be present or they will get a zero, effective leaders consider how to support kids in getting to class. Then, after teachers say students need to be engaged or they'll get a zero, leaders engage the Success Team to support the

Level 2 Systems

Academic Achievement	Behavior Management	Social-Emotional
Academic Support Courses	Community Truancy Boards	Home Visits
Credit Retrieval	Peer Mentors	Resource Management Team

Figure 3.6 Examples of Level 2 interventions.

kids in participating. It's important to consider the input of CoIn teams as students are placed into Level 2 interventions.

A powerful school holds a common understanding: *No* student is a zero. Strong leaders reframe conversations, using common and positive language, to promote support for the student rather than learned helplessness. A combination of interventions from Level 1 and Level 2 systems can be leveraged to offer support to both students and educators.

Academic Support Courses

When students failed to meet standards on state exams, CoIn teams were compelled to respond. They developed what they called tier 2 and tier 3 classes. These courses were designed to have teachers meet standards more intentionally, teach differently, use evidence, and share strategies among themselves. The process of designing them also had an impact on tier 1 classes as teachers considered how to differentiate.

Leaders determined that educators would teach only one additional tiered class so that they would not be overwhelmed, and that when students in the class passed the state exam, they would be awarded credit. Both leaders and teachers are aware of the pressures students feel in these classes. When the leadership team met with the teachers, the teachers spoke up first to remind the formal leaders to "be careful because of the pressure these kids are under." This comment struck the team as funny, given that the meeting had been arranged with the intent of supporting teachers because of the pressure *they* were experiencing.

Credit Retrieval

Credit retrieval should be an assistive factor, but it's best if it's neither a primary go-to intervention nor central to the work of the school. One administrator said of credit retrieval, "We aren't dependent on it, and now we're using it differently." When the turn-

around process began, the school had more than two hundred stations dedicated to credit retrieval for students who were behind
schedule for graduation. Six years later there were less than half as
many stations, and credit retrieval was also being used for online
Advanced Placement physics and other advanced classes; the goal
expanded from a focus on remediation to include acceleration.

Behavior Management

Community Truancy Boards

When students kept not showing up for school, volunteer community members helped students and parents create attendance plans.
Students told the board what the difficulties were that hindered
them in getting to school. The students and the board also created
action plans for improvement, set goals, and met again to follow
up. The truancy board wanted to take the fear out of attendance
issues. With that goal in mind, they capitalized on a powerful vision of networking that included community resources, parent-to-
parent contact, and parent-to-student support.

An additional benefit was that students who went through the
process—participating in a program of strong interventions—generally didn't have to wait as long at the courthouse for proceedings.
Even so, by the time they got there, they were usually in better
shape than they had been when they were initially identified as
needing help, thanks to the intense level of intervention and support
they'd received.

If students were still in jeopardy by the time they reached their
court dates, the court was aware that they had not responded to the
previous levels of intervention provided by the school; therefore,
only students who actually continued to truly need legal interventions were being seen, and those students were bumped to the front
of the line for action.

Peer Mentors

The idea for Peer Mentors came out of the leadership class. Students offered each other support by providing formalized tutoring in various content areas. For example, the strongest math students circulated in ET rooms, while ELL seniors who had met standards on all tests became teaching assistants in ELL courses. These collaborative efforts of students helping students provided social support, affecting such issues as attendance and course pass rates.

Social-Emotional

Home Visits

The appropriate Success Team members went to homes when issues emerged, looking for barriers that students encountered with the hope of providing assistance and resources. Often, they would go multiple times, leaving messages on the door if nobody was home. Over time, parents realized that the home visitor was an advocate, one whom they could contact for support regarding not only academic issues, but also social-emotional needs such as those related to, for example, gang participation or teen pregnancy.

Resource Management Team

A team of counselors, social workers, outside agencies, comprehensive mental health groups, and Child Protective Services formed a Resource Management Team. The team met weekly to access and share data, but only as it related to the school's agenda—the team respected students' and parents' confidentiality. The team helped to connect students and their families with outside resources, including comprehensive mental health services, children's services, drug/alcohol support, probation/parole, and other supports. The school plans to institute an on-campus outpatient treatment program for drugs/alcohol.

LEVEL 3 SYSTEMS

The leadership CoIn team described access to Level 3 systems as a "tight keyhole, monitored closely." Educators want students *on* campus, and they're very reluctant to move them *off* campus. However, certain situations require the move, especially when safety is a factor. In those circumstances, counselors engage more deeply, tending to all three areas—academic achievement, behavior management, and social-emotional development—across the board in each intervention.

Up to this level, this book has presented interventions beneath headings that simplify their focus. At one school, the conversation actually stalled over how to categorize one intervention: Teachers disagreed about whether it should be designated as behavioral or academic.

The fact was, the intervention was needed. What did it matter which heading it was listed under? Although it may feel like a search for clarity, lingering on that kind of distinction may be a way to avoid further work. All interventions should be situated within the conceptual framework. In Level 3, interventions may span the framework. Early on, intensive care in this level might feel burdensome in terms of resources, but it took only a couple of years for the school being discussed.

Academic Achievement, Behavior Management, and Social-Emotional

Bridges

Bridges is an off-campus program focused on getting students who have demonstrated unsafe behaviors back into the mainstream high school. As part of a re-entry program, it works to help students recognize academic barriers in their lives, earn credits through credit retrieval, and negotiate state-mandated testing requirements. Implemented in grades 9 and 10, this is not a program that students

Level 3 Systems

Academic Achievement	Behavior Management	Social-Emotional
Bridges		
Computer-Assisted Learning		

Figure 3.7 Examples of Level 3 interventions.

graduate from; rather, its primary goal is to get students to a place where they can be successfully reintegrated into the school in a safe way.

Computer-Assisted Learning

Primarily for older students in grades 11 and 12, Computer-Assisted Learning (CAL) is an online program used by multiple districts. However, once students are in CAL, the goal is to always bring them back to the schoolhouse. As one administrator noted, even when students are in CAL, "We still consider them *our* kids." CAL can be used as a respite, for a trimester, to address severe behavior disorders or mental health issues.

Keep in mind that no single teacher can "see" the programmatic whole for a student, nor can a student know the entirety of support available. Without the Success Team to oversee all availabilities and appropriately connect students to interventions, the system doesn't function as a whole, and interventions become scattered and disconnected. Additionally, CoIn teams are needed to responsively address classroom needs and communicate them across the system. Only when those two processes (the Success Team and CoIn teams) are functional can the interventions be maximized for all students.

One low-performing school had an isolated intervention program for a select number of students. After the school applied the interventions and principles described here, the interventions were diffused across the entire school within a few years. Now the isolated program doesn't exist—unless it is understood as encompassing the *entire* school.

The bottom line is that all students need support. Isolated programs are insufficient. Entire schools can now be considered the "intervention program," facilitated through the lens shared in this book. Of course these systems can't all be put in place in one year, and, again, they will need to be honed for each individual school. Leaders will find themselves thinking and moving and learning as they go, always remembering to return to the research to refresh their thinking.

SCHOOLWIDE SYSTEMS AND PARENTAL INVOLVEMENT

Once systems are in place, difficult conversations are more easily entered into. Support structures must be present for schools to facilitate partnerships with parents, to help lead the parents regarding what can be done to help their children rather than simply informing them of their failures. Sadly, in schools that are failing, outreach to parents is often perfunctory, applied to pass levees or for other political reasons. In schools where teachers are already overwhelmed, teachers worry about doing genuine outreach with parents because they fear that contact might add to their workload. Many see the parental role as a political and necessary evil rather than as a *lever for change*. However, it is in just these schools that applying servant-leadership principles to relationships with parents is so important.

If teachers, administrators, and students in a school are feeling powerless, the parents of the students are very likely feeling the same way. How can leaders empower parents and help them understand how they fit into the process, creating a greater sense of belonging?

Research suggests that when parents are actively engaged, student learning improves. What is required of parents in terms of collaboration is no different from what's required of all other stakeholders. But if they are to collaborate effectively, parents need the same elements of relational trust the other stakeholders need: to feel safe, to feel that the school has something to offer them, and to believe that the school will put in the time to help them. Without systems grounded in the behavioral, social-emotional, and achievement needs of their child, without a safe environment and the time necessary to meet goals, what does the school have to offer?

Parents want the same thing schools want—for the kids to succeed. Parents want to know that their time is making a difference, that it's really helping their children be successful. A school that is powerless has very little to offer those within the school, let alone parents. It's hard for leaders and teachers at such a school to open the doors and say, "Come on in!" when they feel as if they have nothing to give.

One thing they must have to offer is rich relationships. If the quality of the relationships that kids have with teachers, that teachers have with each other, and that Success Team members and teachers have with parents isn't good, the school is in trouble.

When a school is in trouble, the principal tends to hide—and the students know it. They sense the lack of collegial atmosphere. The feeling of the school becomes one of "every man for himself." Then nobody feels cared about. Students take that attitude home with them, where parents pick up on it.

Administrators at struggling schools may say, "We have to improve communication with parents," but typically the communication they're referring to is one-way. They might say to parents, "Your child has only ten credits. What are you going to do about it?" Parents don't know the answer, and neither do schools. All too often, leaders inform parents about their child's failures rather than asking parents to help them understand the student better and offering systems that will support the child.

Especially in schools where people feel powerless, changes are likely to be only cosmetic—leaders may put up a webpage or put out a newsletter to disseminate information in the name of improving communication with parents. Those measures don't offer the real information parents need.

Parents need specific, one-on-one conversations that allow them to ask questions, be heard, and provide information about their student. In a school that has built relational trust, the communication is more likely to go like this: "Hey, your kid is struggling. Here are some things we have in place, and here's where you fit in." That kind of conversation builds relational trust.

At the same time, relational trust is being developed among staff through role clarity and supportive systems, including CoIn teams. Then systems start to emerge that encourage parents to support this work. They start to work together with the school. The school starts asking questions like, "Can we bring in social agencies? What can we provide?" At the same time, schools ask parents to inform them about the student. "Tell us about your child. What do we need to know?"

The student is also brought to the table. At that point a parent–child–school relationship is developing. The unit becomes a collaborative problem-solving team, because all parties know that schoolwide programs and systems are in place to support the process. A school can have all kinds of activities in place for students, but if they aren't integrated into a systems approach with teachers and counselors and other Success Team members, the activities won't truly support the students.

The systems approach gives parents an opportunity to understand and embrace their role. The reality is, most parents don't want to be involved in curriculum development and governance;

they just want their kids to get a good education. It's the job of leaders to show parents how they can help teachers and administrators deliver that education.

The real contribution parents can make is to help adults at the school understand the unique needs of the student. The more schools support parents in offering that information, the more parents will want to support the school.

Many parents of students at a low-functioning school feel powerless themselves. They're scared of schools, often because they had bad experiences at school when they were students. Or maybe it's because they haven't been invited to contribute in a way that they find meaningful, a way they understand, one that makes them feel safe. They may sit in on a truancy board or some other committee, but often what they're giving is lip service, which is what they feel they're getting from the school.

An excellent way to reassure parents and help them understand their role is to get other adults to show them. Leaders do well to search out the success stories—every school has them—and use them as resources. If schools reach out to that exceptional teacher who has built a powerful relationship with a parent, often as a result of having the same demographics, they can find those parents who trust the school. Often those parents are the quiet ones whose children are doing well even though many components of their lives are not ideal.

To those parents, leaders can say, "We need your help. We need you to go to the parents who don't trust the school to have their best interests in mind, and slowly reengage them." The parents can start telling administrators and teachers how to make inroads. They may join people from the schoolhouse in making home visits, or they may offer to make those visits first to pave the way. It makes sense to have a parent intervene who has had success and has gone down this road. If leaders can get parents helping parents, any threat that they feel from outside agencies goes away. Then the parents who once felt powerless reconnect to the school and partner with it.

This social support makes the parents feel safe. At that point they can contribute from a position of power. They are likely to build relationships and trust with other parents, with administrators, with teachers, and with students, because the school has supports built in at all those levels.

Before schools invite parents in, they need to know where they're going. If schools don't have a clear direction in mind, parents will fill the vacuum and schools will become a delivery system for whatever personal agendas the parents may want to promote. Any agenda that does not support success for students is a distraction.

Leaders do well to take a lot of time to talk with parents in one-on-ones. It's difficult to serve people without knowing what their needs are. The underlying principles and the related behaviors are the same as those leaders use with teachers. Leaders do well to talk to every parent they can—again, especially the ones who have success stories with the school—and then use those stories to talk with other parents.

It's smart to look at key individual stakeholders, business leaders, and other community leaders, but also to take opportunities to educate parents collectively—through the Chamber of Commerce, the Chicano Action Team, Kiwanis—whatever groups are present in the town. Listen to them, and at the same time provide them with a vision that they can fit into. Be careful not to get caught up in politics, personal or townwide.

Go to parents where they work (with discretion) or meet off campus at a place where they will feel comfortable. Look for themes and patterns, which will generally concern (a) behavior management (including concerns that their child isn't being treated fairly), (b) achievement (including, for example, complaints that teachers aren't communicating assignments properly), and (c) social-emotional concerns.

The overarching theme that surfaces is likely to be: "Nobody cares." Before systems of support are implemented, administrators say teachers don't care, teachers say students don't care, and parents say the school doesn't care. Nobody wins in that blame game, but the student is the biggest loser.

Eliminate the blame game. Each person is feeling uncared for and blaming others from his or her unmet need. Find out more about that need and support parents in getting those needs met. Make sure systems are in place to support parents' needs. Work to their sense of belonging. Build their strengths, being intentional in doing so. Collect data, synthesize it, and apply it.

Pockets of excellence always exist, where there are extraordinary efforts by a teacher or a parent. That excellence can't be expected of everyone, which is why it is essential to have systems that support *everyone*. Even if the systems aren't well defined, a difference will be made if the spirit of intent is there. Parents can discern whether staff from the school are there to find an answer or to point a blaming finger.

A school that is working from a conceptual framework can figure out what pieces to put in place to build relational trust and move from the current reality to a new ideal. Mistakes will be made in the process, but eventually the systems will reflect the school's vision. The school will figure out how to systematize the components necessary to meet people's needs. Change will be taking place from the outside in, and people's heads and hearts will be touched and transformed. That's where the magic happens, and there is no doubt that parents, properly approached and supported, will want to be a part of that.

PUTTING IT ALL TOGETHER

To understand how these systems are developed and implemented, a school leader must appreciate the dynamic interaction between the work of formal leaders and the work of the teachers and counselors through collaborative inquiry.

Formal leaders play a critical role in developing what we call the *45-day plan.* The 45-day plan leads to intentional actions, conceived as part of systems development, that align with and support the work of the staff. This is not a school change plan; this is the *leadership plan* that becomes school leaders' version of a *lesson plan.* It describes what each person is going to do to bring the school closer to its goals through systems development. Embedded in each time period are formative assessments, or quick wins.

The idea behind quick wins is that staff can see the leadership team demonstrating new behaviors in doing their work to support staff in doing *their* work in a very short time. The 45-day planning process is a call to action. It is not about what teachers should do differently, but about what formal leaders are willing to do differently to ensure the success of staff and students. This 45-day planning process declares what is important and organizes the necessary processes and structures that implement systems that are grounded in achievement and in the behavioral and social-emotional needs of students—systems that align with the needs of the teacher.

Thus, the leadership team *acts* on their 45-day plan, the success team *monitors* and *connects* teachers and students to system supports, teachers *act* on their CoIn goals, students *engage* in different processes defined by the systems, and parents *regain* hope through specific actions of the school. When leaders provide systems that support students, teachers, and parents, then all involved will reengage in their work with a clarity of purpose that allows the mission of the school to be actualized.

In this book we focused on three interdependent processes that clearly define the roles of stakeholders in the schoolhouse. Part I explained how to reengage teachers in CoIn. Part II described how Success Teams support teachers and students by using evidence to leverage support and help—a form of caring. Part III outlined behavioral, social-emotional, and achievement systems. The relationship among these systems and the way they are guided by leaders executing the 45-day leadership lesson plan is illustrated in Figure 3.8. Together, implemented with the respect and humanness nour-

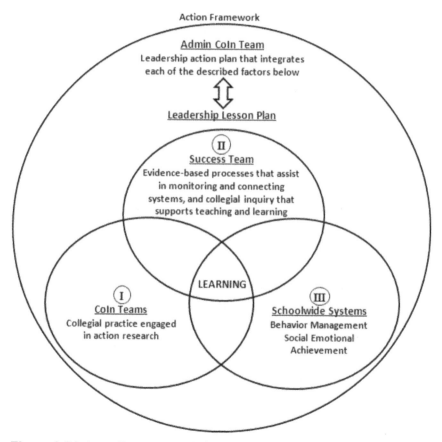

Figure 3.8 Interaction among CoIn teams, Success Team, and schoolwide systems, supported by leadership. These are the actions taken to apply the conceptual framework.

ished by servant-leadership, these systems are likely to increase the
learning of everyone in the schoolhouse.

Conclusion

Though so many schoolhouses are powerless and low-achieving, this status quo is not inevitable. Through applying the conceptual framework in the context of servant-leadership principles, schools can move from powerless to powerful. Academic press, social support, and relational trust implemented through schoolwide systems that support both the adults and the students in the school help everyone move together toward higher academic achievement, building stronger individuals and a stronger organization. Through true collaboration, discerning leadership, a cohesive success team, and practical schoolwide systems, the school begins to transform, and the adults and students in the schoolhouse begin to change their beliefs about what is possible and what they are capable of.

The underlying shifts in beliefs and emotional states that lead to the new way of functioning as a cohesive schoolhouse lay the groundwork for a powerful state in which schools truly serve both the students who are there to learn and achieve, and the adults who help them to do so.

We have had the privilege of seeing schools that were demoralized by low academic achievement, high dropout rates, poverty, parental apathy, low teacher self-efficacy, disciplinary problems, language and cultural barriers, poor attendance, and a general sense of disenfranchisement turn into schools with high academic achievement and a strong sense of unity in which teachers, administrators, and students all bought into the larger mission of the school and felt that they had something to contribute.

In *Powerless to Powerful: Leadership for School Change*, we set out the basic principles that made this change possible. In this book, *Transforming Schools Through Systems Change*, we have offered ideas for implementing the conceptual framework in actionable ways that can transform your schoolhouse from powerless to powerful.

Your school faces unique obstacles and has unique opportunities; use the information in this book while remembering that the resources you need to make your school powerful are *already in the building*.

Find your opportunities for joining forces. Employ the staff you already have to build a Success Team. Implement schoolwide systems that are tailored to your schoolhouse's challenges and needs. The teachers, students, and formal leadership in your building may be frustrated and exhausted right now. That can be the case even in schools with phenomenal staff and students. What you need to know is that the ability to become powerful is already within your reach. It's time to take back our schools by empowering those who do the work. Through a humanistic approach, with relational trust grounded in high expectations and support—change is possible.

Additional Resources

The authors appreciate your efforts to understand the thinking behind this and their previous book, *Powerless to Powerful: Leadership for School Change*, as an effort to engage each other in collective problems of practice and move toward action together in a way that moves everyone closer to the mission of the organization. It is our intent to further support your efforts by developing an implementation guide combining the thinking behind both books to support your good work in schools. Please view our website, www.powerless2powerful.com, for updates, to find further resources, and to share stories of school change.

References

American School Counselor Association. (2012). *The ASCA national model: A framework for school counseling programs* (3rd ed.). Alexandria, VA: Author.

Brookover, W. B., & Lezotte, L. W. (1977). *Changes in school characteristics coincident with changes in student achievement.* East Lansing: Michigan State University, College of Urban Development.

Bryk, A. S., & Schneider, B. (2003). Trust in schools: A core resource for school reform. *Educational Leadership, 60*(6), 40–44. Retrieved from http://www.ascd.org/publications/educational-leadership/mar03/vol60/num06/Trust-in-Schools@-A-Core-Resource-for-School-Reform.aspx.

Covey, S. R. (2013). *The 7 habits of highly effective people: Powerful lessons in personal change* (25th anniversary ed.). New York, NY: Simon & Schuster.

DuFour, R. (2004). *Creating professional learning communities.* Presentation at Washington State ASCD Annual Conference, March 6, Spokane, WA.

DuFour, R., & Eaker, R. (1998). *Professional learning communities at work: Best practices for enhancing student achievement.* Bloomington, IN: Solution Tree.

Edmonds, R. (1979). Effective schools for the urban poor. *Educational Leadership, 37*(1), 15–18, 20–24.

Fulmer, G. W. (2011). Estimating critical values for strength of alignment among curriculum, assessments, and instruction. *Journal of Educational and Behavioral Statistics, 36*(3), 381–402.

Glasser, W. (1998). *The quality school: Managing students without coercion* (3rd rev. ed.) New York, NY: Harper Perennial.

Greenleaf, R. K. (1970). *The servant as leader.* Indianapolis, IN: The Robert K. Greenleaf Center for Servant Leadership. Retrieved from https://www.leadershiparlington.org/pdf/TheServantasLeader.pdf.

Hattie, J. (2009). *Visible learning: A synthesis of over 800 meta-analyses relating to achievement.* New York, NY: Routledge.

Mertler, C. A. (2012). *Action research: Teachers as researchers in the class-room* (3rd ed.). Thousand Oaks, CA: Sage.

Office of Superintendent of Public Instruction. (2005). *School improvement process planning guide.* Retrieved from http://k12.wa.us/StudentAndSchoolSuccess/SIPGuide/SIPGuide.pdf.

Richardson, J. (1999). Norms put the "Golden Rule" into practice for groups. National Staff Development Council. *Tools for Schools,* August/September. Retrieved from http://learningforward.org/docs/tools-for-learning-schools/tools8-99.pdf?sfvrsn=2.

Salina, C., Sylling, E., & Girtz, S. (2016). Curriculum, instruction, assessment (CIA) assessment framework.

Schlegel, J., & Salina, C. (2013). Impact of deep instructional alignment on student achievement. *Curriculum in Context, 39*(1), 22–24.

Spears, L. C. (2000). *Character and servant-leadership: Ten characteristics of effective, caring leaders.* Retrieved from http://www.regent.edu/acad/global/publications/jvl/vol1_iss1/Spears_Final.pdf.

Index

CPSIA information can be obtained
at www.ICGtesting.com
Printed in the USA
LVHW112239100522
718464LV00016B/122

9 781475 822328